GUIDEPOSTS
FOR THE SPIRIT:

Stories of Love for

Mothers

 This Large Print Book carries the
Seal of Approval of N.A.V.H.

GUIDEPOSTS FOR THE SPIRIT:

Stories of Love for

Mothers

EDITED BY
JULIE K. HOGAN

Walker Large Print • Waterville, Maine

Library of Congress Control Number: 2002114803
ISBN 1-4104-0059-X (lg. print : sc : alk. paper)

GUIDEPOSTS
FOR THE SPIRIT:

Stories of Love for

Mothers

CONTENTS

Loving Gestures

*Do not wait for extraordinary
circumstances to do good.
Try to use ordinary situations.*
— JOHANN PAUL FRIEDRICH RICHTER

LOVING GESTURES
MARILYN MORGAN HELLEBERG

A friend whose mother lived with her during the last years of her life wrote in her Christmas letter, "I haven't sent out Christmas cards since 1987, when Mom was still with me. She wanted to help make my life easier, so I set her to work putting stamps and return address stickers on the envelopes. It really saved me a lot of time. She fixed many more envelopes than I needed, and this year when I got out my Christmas things, there they were! So I'm using them and am again being saved a lot of time. Even after her death, she is still making life easier for me."

What a lovely surprise for my friend! It made me wonder what seeds I might plant to be discovered later by those I love. For example, my daughter has a friend who secretly plants bulbs in the yards of her friends. Then, early in the spring, beautiful flowers appear, bringing them great delight and a feeling of being loved.

What could you and I do today to surprise those we love tomorrow? Send someone a magazine subscription without a notification card? Hide love notes in sock drawers, or in the family Bible? Consider it a special secret between God and you. It will make you feel closer to Him, as well as to those you want to surprise!

He who blesses most is blest.
— JOHN GREENLEAF WHITTIER

COUNT YOUR BLESSINGS
LINDA CHING SLEDGE

As a child, I was a precocious worry wart. My mother, seeing my light on late at night, would come into my room sleepy-eyed. "Worrying again?"

"Uh huh," I would nod.

"What about?"

"Well, I didn't do well on the math test today," I would mumble. It wasn't true. But I didn't want to tell her the real reason. I had just changed to a private school and longed to wear cashmere sweaters, just like the other girls. How I worried that they would laugh at my unstylish clothes!

My mother would perch on the edge of my bed, cuddling close. "What's number one on the *Hit Parade*?" she would ask. "When you're tired and you can't sleep," she crooned softly, "count your blessings instead of sheep." Then she would say brightly, "Since you're up, you can do what the song says. Make a 'Bedtime Blessing List.' Writing down all the good things God has given you will put your mind at ease."

It worked. I hadn't realized that my blessings far outnumbered all the material things I felt I lacked. My blessings snaked down one page and across another. Before long my hand was tired, my eyes heavy, and it was all I could do to ask Mother to turn out the light.

*When it comes to life, the critical thing is
whether you take things for granted or
take them with gratitude.*
— G. K. CHESTERTON

BIRTHDAY FLOWERS
GLENN KITTLER

One day I was walking with a friend. As we
approached a florist shop, he stopped to buy
his mother some flowers.

"Is it her birthday?" I asked.

"No," he replied, "it's mine. I send her
flowers as a way to thank her for giving me
life and for taking care of me all those
years until I could take care of myself."

I thought that was a very touching gesture. I had always sent my mother a gift on
her birthday and at Christmas, but it had
never occurred to me to send her anything
on my birthday. So the next time my
birthday came around, I sent my mother
flowers.

That evening she telephoned. "What's

14

all this about?" she asked.

"It's my birthday," I said.

"I know that. Did you get my card?"

"Yes," I said. "Thanks. And the flowers are just to thank you for giving me life and taking care of me all those years until I could take care of myself."

Silence. I could almost see her fighting back the tears. Then, in that way she has always had of brushing aside gratitude and praise, she said, "Well, I'm glad you finally noticed."

Riches take wings, comforts vanish, hope
withers away, but love stays with us.
— LEW WALLACE

LOVE NOTES
PENNEY SCHWAB

One Valentine's Day my daughter Rebecca handed me a slip of paper. "Look in the blue vase on your dresser," it instructed. I looked, and found another note: "See what's hidden in your jewelry box." A third note was wrapped around a necklace, this one directing me to reach under my pillow. I did, and pulled out a red construction paper heart. On it Rebecca had drawn a picture of the two of us, hand in hand. "I love you!" she'd printed in big, bold letters.

Rebecca's love notes prompted me to search for some tangible ways of sharing my love. I telephoned my foster brother in California to say, "I wish we could be together more often." I made raisin "valentines" on the kids' cereal. (They thought it

16

was silly, but liked it.) I invited an elderly friend who lives alone to be my "mother" for the church Mother-Daughter Banquet.

Are there love notes you can share? They'll be appreciated not only on Valentine's Day, but throughout the year. Why, you might even surprise your child (or parent or spouse) with a treasure hunt that ends with a special expression of your love!

Every gift which is given, even though it be small, is great if given with affection.
— Pindar

The Lunch Box
Marion Bond West

In the early 1960s my husband and I became the parents of two little girls, two years apart. Quiet, obedient, demure children. I quickly assumed the role of a confident, smiling mother, with enormous time, energy, and enthusiasm — even patience.

When the girls approached eight and six, twin sons arrived. Superactive, loud, demanding, headstrong. Julie, my oldest little girl, became my faithful helper, folding mounds of diapers, strolling the babies, helping her sister, Jennifer, get ready for school, reading to all the children while I prepared meals. I could always depend on her, and I did. Perhaps too much.

The carefree days the girls and I had known vanished abruptly. Supermom dis-

18

integrated bit by bit, and a tired, grim woman replaced her. Sometimes I cried silently from sheer weariness. Julie often saw me and tried even harder to help. She never complained.

It was only after Julie was grown and married that I learned of the hurt she'd felt back then. One day she laughingly asked me, "Remember my school lunches you made, Mom? All my friends took their lunches in cute little lunch boxes, and I wanted to be like them. Did you know I was embarrassed to eat with my friends? Those fancy lunch boxes of theirs were always filled with wonderful things their mothers had put in them."

I leaned forward, our faces inches apart, listening intently. Julie somehow seemed to have become a child again. "Jeannie's lunches were always the best. She had little sandwiches cut into halves, triangles, and circles, and packed in small sandwich bags. She had neat little carrot sticks! She always had a folded napkin for whatever holiday was approaching.

"On cold days Claire had hot soup or hot cocoa in a thermos. And their mothers often tucked notes in their lunch boxes . . ."

I listened to Julie, fascinated, as she went on. "Sometimes, Mom, you threw a couple of unwashed, unpeeled carrots in a sack — the largest sack I'd ever seen — and spread peanut butter on two hard pieces of bread, and threw in an old apple and a crumbling cookie. I folded the sack forever, trying to make it small."

"Why didn't you ever tell me?" I asked, a ball of sorrow beginning to form in my stomach.

She laughed a genuine laugh, and appeared grown-up again. "You were so busy. I could see you were trying as hard as you could with the boys, and you just never got caught up. I knew you were always tired. Anyway, Jen and I had cute clothes with matching hair ribbons. You always helped us with posters, and picked us up when we had to stay late at school and couldn't ride the bus. Remember the raincoats you bought us with matching umbrellas?" She tried very hard to make it okay. After all these years, she was still committed to helping me.

I couldn't drop the subject. "What was it like when the lunch bell rang?"

"Well . . . I always dreaded lunch. I hid my sack under some stuff in the cloak room and always . . . hoped that maybe. . . ." She brightened. "Once, I found a grocery ticket in the bottom of my sack and for a moment . . . I thought you'd written a note."

"I never knew you wanted a lunch box," I spoke in a whisper of regret.

Years passed, and from time to time I thought of the lunch box Julie had yearned for years ago. In my mind, she sat alone in a corner of the lunchroom while her friends chatted away eating dainty sandwiches and reading notes from their mamas.

Last September, Julie's two little girls were in kindergarten and second grade. She phoned to tell me they'd just got on the school bus for the first day of school. "Mama, they picked out their own lunch boxes. Jamie's is pink and Katie's is yellow. I made their lunches last night." Excitement spilled through the telephone, filling my kitchen and my heart. "Triangle sandwiches, Mama, with the edges trimmed. M & M's. Grapes. Cheese. Homemade cookies. A drumstick . . . everything in separate bags."

"Julie, Julie!" I screamed into the phone. "Did you remember the notes?"

"Yes. Oh, yes!" she responded.

One day I was fervently cleaning out the garage. I reached down to the bottom of a dusty cardboard box and pulled out some-

21

thing. A tin lunch box! On the front was a lovable smiling television tiger. I sat cross-legged on the garage floor and held the lunch box tenderly on my lap.

Dear Lord, is it possible that you're giving me a second chance?

Go ahead, a silent voice urged. *It's not too late.*

I took the lunch box to the kitchen sink and washed it as carefully as if it were crystal. What does a mother put in a lunch box for a daughter who lives a thousand miles away? Mounds candy bars, Life Savers, gum, a little box of raisins!

Remembering Julie's passion for old, sentimental things, I included some paper dolls, an antique lace handkerchief, and a very old hand-embroidered tea towel. Such a tiny space to pack in so much . . . love. I tucked in a jeweled hair comb and a small book about friendship published in the early 1900s. In this book, I printed, "Julie, pretend this is a washed, peeled carrot, cut up properly."

In a tiny satin container, I enclosed an antique pin a friend had given me years ago. Some small packages of Julie's favorite cosmetics and hair products also went into the lunch box. When it would hold no more, I carefully placed a folded napkin on the top — a napkin with a big brown turkey and golden leaves and the words "Happy Thanksgiving." Of course I'd hidden a note in the very bottom of the lunch box.

Driving to the post office with the carefully wrapped package, I reasoned joyfully (if not logically): Never mind that the lunch box is over twenty years late. Never mind that Julie is almost thirty. At last, she was about to have a lunch box! *Please Lord, don't let it be too late,* I prayed.

Three days later the phone rang. I didn't recognize the voice at first. Someone was squealing, laughing, crying. "Mother, I never realized that I'm still seven years old. It was so . . . emotionally heavy I could barely breathe. When I opened the lunch box it was just as though I was sitting at the long table and all my friends were watching me!"

"So the lunch box wasn't too late, after all?" I croaked.

"Too late? Oh, never." Then she paused. "Most of all, though, I loved the note you put at the bottom. Back in the second grade, Mama, maybe I wished for a triangle-shaped sandwich or a peeled carrot stick, and, especially, a note. But I always knew you loved me, Mother."

23

*He that does good to another
does good to himself.*
— SENECA

HELPING OTHERS
PATRICIA LORENZ

The most wonderful card I ever received was the handmade, beautifully painted Father's Day card my daughter Jeanne sent me for Father's Day a few years after I became a single parent. I'd been both mother and father to her, she wrote, and she just wanted me to know how much she appreciated it.

Mother's Day is generally an event orchestrated by fathers. They take the kids shopping and help them buy gifts and flowers for Mom. Some husbands take their wives out for brunch to celebrate her special day. But when there's no dad around, a single mom is lucky if a thoughtful teacher has organized the making of a Mother's Day card during art class.

Think about all the single-parent moms you know. Think about how Mother's Day is in some way the most important day of the year for them, because they aren't wives anymore — only mothers. And they usually do it while holding down full-time jobs and trying to make ends meet.

Ask if you can "borrow" the children of a single-parent mom for a few hours. Take them shopping for gifts for their mother — not expensive ones, but something she can unwrap excitedly. Help the children wrap the gifts, if necessary. The children will be excited about the whole idea. But that mother — she'll appreciate it more than you can imagine.

Children are an heritage of the Lord . . .
— PSALM 127:3

GRANDMOTHER'S PIN
FAY ANGUS

My grandmother's pin is pale gold, embedded with twelve opalescent seed pearls. These glow from a crescent moon that tips upward to a shining star, with a little diamond that flickers light as from a secret hiding place.

She wore it nearly always. She touched it sometimes, as though to pull from it faith and courage. . . . to keep on dreaming.

Now the pin was mine. She gave it to me years ago folded in plain white tissue on which she had written in a shaky hand: "You are sweet sixteen — it's time for moonglow, dancing stars, and promises of dreams come true!"

I have treasured it and worn it, through the years, nearly always. Sometimes I tuck it into my pocket, easy to the touch of my tired hands and tired heart, so in need of promises.

A few years back, I wrapped the pin in plain white tissue on which I wrote to my daughter Katrelya:

This Valentine's Day, my darling daughter, you are sweet sixteen — time for moonglow, dancing stars, and the promises of dreams come true! Your great-grandmother's pin . . . wrapped in tissue . . . once given to me, now a token of remembrance and love passed along to you!

*Virtue is to the soul
what health is to the body.*
— FRANCOIS, DUC DE LA ROCHEFOUCAULD

MAMA'S SPIRITUAL SCRAPBOOK
ELENORE KNOX

There I was, stumped, right in the middle of sorting out and disposing of my mother's possessions. Her furniture posed no real problem, and her clothes we could give away easily, but what was I to do with all these odd little personal items Mama had collected over the years? What about these clippings from her church paper, or this bookmark with The Lord's Prayer on it, or the Rose of Sharon pin her friend had brought home from the Holy Land? These oddments would mean precious little to anybody else, I thought. Even so, I couldn't bear to throw them out.

"I'll make a scrapbook!" I told my husband suddenly. "I'll gather together all these bits and scraps that were meaningful to Mama, and I'll paste them in one giant book."

It took me a long time, but that's exactly what I did, until I had a big book bulging with such things as a letter from the minister who had married Mama; a silver coin showing praying hands and an inscription that read, "With God all things are possible"; "An Indian Prayer" written on birch bark; a cross woven from a Palm Sunday frond — all mementos of God's love. Gradually I began to add items of my own, and whenever I took out the scissors and paste to make another entry, I had the feeling that Mama was there, looking over my shoulder.

And then came that ugly day when my doctor told me I had cancer. Immediate surgery would be necessary, he said.

What a terrible enemy fear can be! Suddenly my faith was gone and despair took over. I loved this life and the husband, children, and grandchildren I shared it with. I didn't want to lose it. First came, "I don't believe it." Then, "It isn't fair!" And finally, worst of all, "There is no God."

At home that afternoon, my husband came to me as I sat in the armchair staring worriedly into space. Silently he placed the big scrapbook in my shaking hands, and almost involuntarily I opened it. My eyes fell on words Mama had loved, carefully copied from the twelfth chapter of Isaiah: "Behold, God is my salvation; I will trust, and not be afraid: for the LORD Jehovah is my strength and my song; he also is become my salvation" (Isaiah 12:2).

Slowly peace flowed back on a stream of renewed faith. Panic faded. God would take care of me. It seemed as though Mama herself were there, reassuring me once again that God was with me and that everything would be all right.

Two years have passed since then. I am completely recovered. But just to be sure, I keep Mama's spiritual scrapbook handy. It's the life insurance Mama left me.

The Lord watch between me and thee,
when we are absent from one another.
— GENESIS 31:49

LONG-DISTANCE LOVE
CAROL KUYKENDALL

I keep this silly picture of my daughter Lindsay on my desk — her hair covered with confetti — to remind me to cover her with long-distance love this year while she's away at college. I snapped the picture just before hugging her good-bye at the end of a welcoming ceremony when clouds of confetti rained down on a roomful of jittery freshmen, a symbolic gesture of "covering them with love."

When I got home and looked at this picture, I began to think of ways I could cover her with love . . . in spite of our physical separation. For ideas, I turned to the Apostle Paul, the "Master of Long-Distance Loving." According to Scripture, Paul used two methods of communicating

31

his love to new believers: he prayed for them regularly (and told them so); and he wrote letters.

So I joined a Mothers' Prayer Group, which meets regularly to share requests and pray for our kids far away from home. I purchased a supply of stationery, knowing that something — anything — fills an empty mailbox with a tangible message of love. Sometimes I send her a picture postcard from home or jot down a few "Proverbs from Mom" (starting with "Proverbs 32" since the Bible has 31). Obviously, my messages are not as deep as Paul's, but I hope my gestures of long-distance love are just as real.

Honour thy father and thy mother.
— EXODUS 20:12

VISITING MOTHER
BETTY L. MILLS

For almost seven years I've been visiting my mother in a nursing home. She no longer recognizes me and just rambles on, not making any sense.

Lately I have been visiting her during my lunch hours in order to see her while she is awake. I often return to work upset and frustrated. One day a fellow worker said, "Oh, Betty, you're so lucky!"

"Lucky?" I retorted. "My mother doesn't even know who I am."

"But you know who *she* is," my friend answered. "My mother died when I was twelve, and I'd give anything now if I could kiss her and tell her I love her. You can do that."

I had never thought about it that way, and since that day my attitude toward my visits has changed. Mother, now almost ninety, still rambles on, but while she does, I pat her hands, I kiss her, and I tell her I love her. And sometimes there is joy, when she speaks her few understandable words — "Bless you. Thank you for coming."

Words of Patience

Patience and silence go together.
— PARAMANANDA

TWIST AND SHAPE GENTLY
SUE MONK KIDD

It was past her bedtime. I'd told her not once, but three times to get into bed. But there she was, still sitting on the floor of her room, blowing up balloons and twisting them into assorted shapes. Earlier I'd bought my eleven-year-old daughter a "Balloon Craft" kit with a step-by-step instruction book on creating everything from a giraffe to a dachshund. She'd been captivated by it for hours to the point of ignoring me. Aggravated, I planted my fists on my hips. "Ann, get in bed and do it now!" I shouted.

She jumped. *Bam!* the blue balloon exploded in her hands. She stared at me as if her face, too, were about to shatter.

As she climbed into bed, I picked up the

menagerie of balloons from the floor, then bent down to retrieve the book of instructions. That's when my eyes fell upon the bold print at the top of the page: "Twist and shape the figures *gently* to avoid popping."

I paused and looked at the little "figure" curled beneath the sheets. "I'm sorry I shouted at you," I whispered. Then I brushed back the brown bangs on her forehead ever so gently.

Know thine opportunity.
— PITTACUS

ADVICE FROM MOM TO MOM
CAROL KUYKENDALL

"Kendall, I will *never ever* do this again," I vowed through clenched teeth to my thirteen-year-old daughter as we scraped paper off the walls of her bedroom. Pulling this little-girl paper off and putting up something more appropriate for a teenager represented a rite of passage for Kendall and she was clearly excited. But I detested the tedious task and had been complaining for two solid days as we worked away.

The next day, I ran into the mother of a friend of Kendall's. She asked what we'd been up to lately. I related an exaggerated story of the pains of peeling wallpaper.

"Oh, Mandy and I did that a few weeks ago," she answered. "We laughed and talked about growing up . . . stuff we never sit down and discuss. I was glad for the opportunity."

We parted laughing, but as I turned to walk away, I was almost in tears. Same job. Different attitude. And certainly, a different result: She seized upon an opportunity I totally missed because of my whining and complaining.

I wonder if Martha felt the same regret when she realized she missed the opportunity of sitting at the feet of Jesus because of her fussing and complaining. I also wonder if Kendall might like to re-wallpaper her room again in a couple of years. Then again, maybe we'll find other opportunities . . .

If you would judge, understand.
— SENECA

TEEN FOR A DAY
KAREN BARBER

We had just moved and I was dropping off my tenth grader, Chris, at his school. I was ready to leave, but he wasn't. Chris's brown bangs flopped across his forehead as he jerked away in annoyance. "Mom, we're leaving too early. You just don't understand!"

Tension crept into my neck. Now that Chris was a teenager, at times I felt like I was attempting to communicate with a being from another planet and not with the fun-loving offspring I had been raising for the past fifteen years. "What is there to understand?" I shot back. "In case there's traffic we need to leave at 7:45."

"I can't hang around all by myself before the bell," Chris mumbled.

"We're not risking being late for such a

42

ridiculous reason," I answered. We left promptly at 7:45 a.m.

The following week Chris staggered in from school and dumped his backpack with a thump that made me frown. When I asked him about his classes, it became clear he hadn't been participating in class discussions. "Chris," I argued, "you have good ideas."

"But none of the other kids say anything."

So what? I wrinkled my forehead. Maybe I was the one who just wasn't getting it. *Why won't a smart kid speak up in class?*

That weekend I overheard Chris telling his brother he had shoved someone in the halls. "Chris!" I horned in. "How could you do such a thing?"

"You don't know how crowded it is," he protested. "The guy was in my way and he was just standing there talking to somebody."

"Don't ever do that again!" I scolded. Chris turned and stomped off to his room. As his stereo blasted, I prayed, *Lord, what does it take to understand a teenager?*

The first week in October I received a notice about the school's "Wacky Tuesday." Parents were invited to attend school in place of their teenagers and the teenagers were to go to their parents' place of work. There were rules: Each parent had to stay for the entire day and take notes for his or her child. Apparently, several dozen parents did it every year. It sounded interesting, so I signed up.

The day before Wacky Tuesday, I told Chris, "This afternoon when I pick you up I want you to show me how to find all your classes."

"No way, Mom. Nobody showed me around the first day. I want you to know exactly how I felt."

"Fine," I answered, thinking, *What on earth has gotten into him?*

On Wacky Tuesday, Chris put on a shirt and a tie and went to the office with my husband, Gordon. I pulled on a turtleneck, slacks, and running shoes. I heaved a backpack crammed with Chris's books over my shoulders, and was off to high school at a quarter to eight.

Inside the school with time to spare and no one to talk to, I stood uncomfortably, listing under the weight of the backpack.

Okay, I'd try to make sense of the map the school had given out. I had to get to room 5109, placed for some reason on the first level.

I plunged into a traffic jam of students,

gym duffels, and open lockers and turned down the wrong hall. I raced to correct my course and found the stairway blocked by a girl with a gargantuan book bag. As the girl prattled mindlessly with some friends, I thought, *This kid is as effective a roadblock as a hippopotamus.*

I elbowed my way through oncoming traffic, not bothering to say excuse me as I rushed.

In Algebra II the teacher handed out a graded exam and went through the solutions on the blackboard. She wrote so fast I could barely copy the figures down. It was a scene from a nightmare: I walk into an exam and haven't the foggiest notion how to do anything.

The knot in my stomach tightened during second and third periods. In Geography, the kids working on our project responded to my suggestions with blank stares. In Keyboarding, the lesson was on keys I rarely used.

Lunch was next. There were several empty places, but I hesitated. *What if they're saving those places for their friends? Or don't want me around?* Finally I spotted a bunch of parents and practically sprinted to an empty spot at their table.

I had been looking forward to English,

and had eagerly read the assigned pages in *Lord of the Flies*. The teacher asked the class how they envisioned the forest fire the boys carelessly start. Such details don't matter — the book is more of a parable than a news account, I wanted to say. For some reason my hand stayed firmly by my side. Maybe the teacher is about to make that point and I'd steal his thunder. Or maybe I'll sound show-offy or stupid and the others will laugh at me.

Biology was my last class, and it was lab day. We frantically measured and cut straws into various lengths to represent differing ionization rates. The final bell rang just when I read the rather odd last question on the lab sheet: "What did you learn about yourself in this lab?"

I gathered my books and plunged into the frantic hall. I'm not fighting those hippopotamuses through the crowded halls just to stash these in Chris's locker, I decided. Instead, I fled out the nearest exit.

My car was parked three blocks away. By the second block the backpack straps cut into my shoulders and my lower back was screaming out that I was, after all, a middle-aged woman. When I walked through the kitchen door and threw down that book bag, I felt a thousand pounds lighter. So this is how Chris feels when he gets home.

Suddenly I found myself mentally filling in that last question on the biology lab sheet. I had done everything I had been criticizing Chris for. At lunch I had dreaded sitting with strangers. In English class I had kept quiet. And in my panic to get to class on time I had done some aggressive pushing.

When Chris got home from his dad's office he looked at his stuffed book bag and groaned. "Don't tell me I have that much homework!"

"You don't," I explained sheepishly. "I didn't feel like fighting the hippopotamuses to get to your locker. High school's hard work. I'm glad I got to see what you have to deal with."

"Yep." Chris's nonchalant shrug could mean "typical parent, stating the obvious again." But I could see the shrug went along with a look in his eye that meant my fun-loving offspring was communicating, "Well, Mom finally gets it."

I grinned. Yes, I finally "got" not just my teenager, but also what the Book of Proverbs has been teaching parents for thousands of years: "Be ye of an understanding heart" (Proverbs 8:5).

As every thread of gold is valuable,
so is every minute of time.
— JOHN MASON

THE IMPORTANCE OF
LIGHTNING BUGS
PAM KIDD

"Want to take an after-dinner walk?" my husband asks.

"With half the house left to clean?" I protest. To further make my point, I yell down the hall. "Brock! Keri! Don't even think of going to bed until your rooms are clean!"

"Oh, Mama," Keri replies, "we were going to catch lightning bugs."

An hour later, I scan my "things-to-do" list, and see that the house is reasonably clean. I think of Keri's lightning bugs, and I recall childhood's cool grass under bare feet and the fresh watermelon smell that hung in the air as I ran through the night reaching for stars.

I walk across the porch and sit on the top step. In the simple dark I take stock. Do I really want my children to know me as a grouchy mom with a very clean house?

I hurry inside, take four empty jars from under the sink, and call my glum family of house-cleaners together. "I have a problem with lightning bugs," I say. "I need to see if it's still fun to catch them on a summer night." And then, because confession brightens the soul, I add, "I think it might be more important than a clean house."

It was. It still is.

Cheerfulness is the atmosphere
in which all things thrive.
— JOHANN PAUL FRIEDRICH RICHTER

MOTORIZED MOTHER
PATRICIA LORENZ

"I'm tired of spending my whole life in that car," I grumbled, scowling as I grabbed the car keys off the kitchen counter. My son Michael had just reminded me that we had to go out to buy his basketball shoes that evening.

"I'm averaging two hundred miles a week just driving you kids to games, lessons, rehearsals, shopping, cheerleading practice, and taking you to friends' houses! Two hundred miles a week and nobody cares!" My voice faded when I realized nobody was listening.

As a single parent, I was the one to do the driving whenever the four kids needed to be driven somewhere.

"Mom, don't forget there's the dance at

school tonight," Julie reminded.

Back home from that jaunt, I collapsed in front of the TV to read the newspaper, when suddenly six-year-old Andrew was at my side. "Mommy, can we go to the store now?"

"No, dear, not now," I said wearily.

"But your birthday's tomorrow," Andrew whimpered.

Ah, yes, my birthday. I'd forgotten. I'd promised to take him shopping. He'd been saving his nickels and dimes to buy me a present. He'd decided upon earrings and expected me to help pick them out.

"All right, Andrew," I said. "Let me put my shoes back on and get ready. We'll go now."

How do you say no to such a big heart implanted in such a little body?

At the store we browsed among the carousel of earrings. Andrew pointed to a pair he liked. I told him they were beautiful. (They were also on sale for three dollars, a dollar less than what was in his cowboy coin purse.)

Knowing he'd made up his mind, I said, "Andrew, decide what you want to do while I go over here and buy socks for Michael." I knew he needed to be alone.

From the next aisle I could hear his

pride-filled voice saying, "Yes, please," when the lady asked him if he needed a box for the earrings. "It's my mom's birthday and I'm going to wrap them in red paper with white hearts."

After a stop for an ice-cream cone, we headed home, and Andrew disappeared into his room with the red paper and a roll of tape.

"Get your pajamas on, honey; then come to my room and we'll read your bedtime story in my bed."

When he jumped in the bed, Andrew snuggled close to me.

"Mommy, this is the happiest day of my life!"

"Why is that, honey?"

"It's the first time I've ever been able to do anything for you!" Then his arms surrounded me in a spontaneous bear hug.

While Andrew plodded out loud through one of his first-grade readers, I thought about my own acts of giving. I was always giving to my children — especially in the car. Yet somehow I was never happy about it.

Later I tucked this little boy with the big heart into his bed. "What about prayers, Mom?"

I'd forgotten. "Oh, of course, honey."

I held Andrew's hands in mine and thanked God for my small son — and for all my children. I asked God to help me be a more cheerful mother.

Later I looked up the verse that had been running through my head, the one about God loving a cheerful giver (2 Corinthians 9:7).

Then and there I decided to stop being such a grouch about the driving. And as I became something I thought I'd never be, a cheerful chauffeur, I found that I was listening to things I'd never quite heard before. On the way to band practice or drum lessons, Michael, age fourteen, thought out loud about whether he should go out for football. He also told me about the girl in his class who had called him the night before, discussed whether he should get a job after school, and talked about what he wanted to do with his life.

When Julie, age fifteen, was in the car with me, she bubbled on and on about the latest antics in her cheerleading squad, about the boy who'd asked her to homecoming, about the student council fundraiser, and about getting extra help in geometry.

On the way to Jeanne's piano lessons, confirmation classes, and a special event downtown at the Milwaukee High School of the Arts, where she was a senior, we talked about where she wanted to go to college, what was happening in her art classes, and why she felt her social life was at a standstill.

Amazed by what I'd missed as a cranky mom, I began looking forward to wheeling around town with my four kids in tow. Given a chance, the kids opened up. We laughed together, debated, questioned, shared our feelings, and grew much closer. I still drive two hundred miles a week, but I look forward to every mile, because driving time has become family time in our car. Prime time. Time for giving, cheerfully.

*No gift to your mother can ever equal
her gift to you — life.*
— AUTHOR UNKNOWN

ON MOTHERHOOD
KATRINA KENISON

As mothers, we are bound by depths of pain and waves of joy that those who have not raised children will never know. In each of our children we see a miracle of life — even as we realize, with sudden insight, that the world is full of just such miracles. I called my own mother at three a.m. — as the obstetrician sat on a stool between my legs, stitching my episiotomy with long black thread — and told her she was a grandmother. An hour and a half later, she slipped into my room, having driven alone in the dark, without directions, to a city hospital she had never seen before. She talked her way past the security guards and the night nurses, and she came to me. I was not altogether surprised to see her, though; it was just beginning to dawn on me what it means to be a mother . . .

Overnight the world had changed. I felt like a traveler who sets foot on foreign soil only to realize that she has journeyed to the right place after all, that she has found home. Settling into this new home meant coming to know myself as a mother, discovering my child, and, with my husband, enlarging our marriage to include and embrace a third . . . When I joined the tribe of mothers, the experiences of mothers everywhere became, in some measure, my own.

Dost thou love life?
Then do not squander time;
for that's the stuff life is made of.
— BENJAMIN FRANKLIN

THE FULLNESS OF LIFE
LYNN COLWELL

I rolled over in bed and instinctively reached for the small spiral notebook. Every morning for six years, I'd done the same thing — reached for my marching orders, my neatly printed list of things to do that day. Steve always teased me about my prearranged schedule, but if I didn't organize the night before, how else would I get through the logjam of work each day?

This morning the notation CLEAN HALL CLOSET stood like a glowering general at the top of my list. Dispiritedly, I began picking through mismatched shoes, games with missing pieces, and boxes of unmarked photographs. Then I saw the hammock. It lay in a tangled heap. I recalled how we had laughed, Steve and I, when my brother gave it to us. Except for two very spindly trees, our property was barren then. So we had thanked him and swiftly abandoned the useless gift in the back of the closet. But now, glancing out the window, I saw the two sturdy trees that had grown from those reedy transplants. Then I surprised myself by stepping out into the blinding sunlight. I stood on tiptoe and carefully stretched the hammock between the two strong trunks.

At a glance, one could see this was not an ordinary canvas hammock, but an artfully woven cocoon formed from thousands of red and yellow cords. Within its eleven-foot arc, there was room for a couple of adults or several children to nestle, weightless above the grass.

The baby's agitated cry broke my reverie. Corey was hungry. I was quite adept at nursing while holding her in one arm like a football and using my free arm to dust or vacuum. *But just this once,* I thought guiltily, *we'll rest in the hammock.*

I backed into it and brought in my legs so that Corey and I settled like birds in a swinging nest. The swaying soothed us both, and Corey nursed as I sought the clouds through the leafy canopy. The world was empty of human sound, but I heard a woodpecker rat-a-tat-tatting and the wind rustling the leaves. A humming-bird spied a flower and, swooping down, it fed daintily, its wings a blur. I felt completely at peace. But then, the feeling of guilt: God's world would be here to-morrow, but the baby needed clean diapers today!

At three o'clock I heard the slow foot-steps of my six-year-old son. I looked up from folding diapers and noticed his for-lorn face.

"What's up, Chris?" I asked.

"Oh, nothing," he replied, unwilling to talk.

"Look," I said, pointing through the window, "a surprise for you."

"Wow! That's neat," he exclaimed. "Can we get in it?"

His small face reflected such happiness that I resisted the urge to say "Not right now," and together we walked outside and slipped into the hammock's embrace. I reached over and put an arm around my son. I hadn't held him that close in a long time, and I was surprised he didn't pull away.

"You know what happened in school today?" Chris asked plaintively. "That big kid Robbie Simmons has been picking on me, pushing me down, calling me names. Today in front of all the other guys, he pulled, well, he tried to pull my pants down. Then I . . ." Muffled sobs shook the hammock. I was furious at that bully, but strangely I felt happy too. Lying snug in the hammock, Chris had opened his heart to me. That contained little boy, who rarely spoke his feelings, was trusting me with that fragile part of himself.

That evening Steve dragged in from work looking exhausted. After the children were in bed, I gently led him outside to see the hammock. We couldn't help but lie together and watch the moon rise in the black sky. Soon, swaying in the silent night, old dreams awakened. The pressures of every day had kept our dream-talk dormant. Now we talked away the night and felt closer than we had in a long, long time.

The next morning I awoke to the sound of thunder. Lightning flashed angrily, and rain poured out of a cast-iron sky. I glanced at my bedside table, and on it was a note in Steve's handwriting: "Please put the hammock on your list for tonight!"

I laughed to myself, but with the next bolt of lightning, I saw a clear vision of myself suspended above the earth with Corey at my breast, and I could hear myself thinking, *God's world will be here tomorrow, but the baby needs clean diapers today!* True, God's world was here today, but it was stormy and bleak, not a good day for lying in a hammock and relishing the smell and touch of one's young. Yesterday was the day to listen to the unburdening of a small heart and to nurture dreams.

I had learned my lesson. For several moments I followed the raindrops on their winding journey down the windowpane and said a quiet *Thank you* to God for the fullness of life that he offers us — if we are ready to accept it. Then I tore up my list of jobs for the day and called to the children, "Let's run out and taste the rain!"

*A world without children
is a world without newness,
regeneration, color, and vigor.*
— JAMES C. DOBSON

MY WORST
MOTHER'S DAY EVER
DEBORAH SMOOT

It was Mother's Day, so our little church was
packed. At the door, an usher handed a
long-stemmed pink carnation to every female who qualified. ("Are you a mother?" he
would ask.)

My arms were already full with my four-
year-old's coat and a diaper bag for my
one-year-old. Shifting those things onto
my right arm, I held the carnation above
my head so it wouldn't get smashed, then
made my way to a pew where my husband
and parents were sitting.

There would be no surprises in the program, I thought. It was the same every year

— a sea of pink carnations, eulogies to motherhood and, of course, songs about mommies sung by children who wiggled throughout the program.

But this year a well-meaning Sunday-school teacher had come up with a better idea. She asked each child to draw a picture of his mother, and she made these into slides. After each song, a slide of someone's mother was shown, and the child who had drawn the picture was handed the microphone.

"This is my mommy driving the car. She takes us places." A picture of a happy mom with a smiling red crayon mouth, looking out of a car window, flashed on the screen behind the pulpit.

"This is my mom cooking dinner." Mom with yellow hair and a ruffled apron came into focus. It was a nice touch.

The drawings varied in detail, but all were sweet and tender. As my turn approached, I grew more and more eager. I knew my four-year-old's drawing would be something wonderful — his mommy standing, say, in a field of flowers.

I was somewhere in the middle of that fantasy when I heard Owen bellow: "This is my mommy washing clothes when she first gets up in the morning." The audience roared with laughter at the drawing on the screen. Like a real pro, Owen waited for the laughter to die down before he added, "But I didn't get her hair right. It sticks up more than that."

I could have died. Guilt took the seat next to me, and self-doubt sat next to him. *Is that really how Owen sees me? Should I jump out of bed an hour before everyone else, dress, comb my hair, apply lip gloss?*

Before I became a mother, I was downright sure of myself about mothering. When Dave and I were newlyweds, his brother and sister-in-law brought their small boys for Easter dinner. The boys got bored and crawled under the table, under the piano, in and out of adult legs. Later I commented to my husband that when we had children, they would never crawl under the piano; I would bring things for them to do, so they wouldn't be bored. I foresaw color-coded bags hanging on hooks in our garage — each full of new crayons and age-appropriate activities — bags I could grab at a moment's notice so my children would always be happy, learning, never bored.

Now, thirteen years into mothering, and having had a few of my own children under the piano, I realize how naive I was. My bag consists of a few graham crackers I grab on the way out the door. With three children — Owen is now thirteen, Emily ten, and Amy six — I'm into survival.

Motherhood is, at best, a humbling experience. Just the other day, Amy ran into the kitchen with two friends in tow and said, "Mom, you gotta laugh! I told them you have the silliest laugh. You have to let them hear it, so they'll believe me. Laugh, Mom, laugh!"

I've always admired humility in others. I just had no idea the price they paid for it.

A friend tells of an executive and his wife who would come to dinner parties and give their "ten commandments for parenting." Soon they had their first baby, then number two, and they came to parties with "eight rules for parenting." By the time they were raising three teenagers, they had gone from "ten commandments" to "three suggestions."

That's about where I am on this Mother's Day: three suggestions that *might* work, not just for parenting, but for life in general. After all, what are children but small people?

1. *Listen.* My Aunt Lois always listened to us children no matter what kind of question we had. With everyone else, we

kids talked mostly to kneecaps or belt buckles. But whenever we approached Aunt Lois, we didn't get just an answer, we got Aunt Lois. She would hunker down nose-to-nose with us. We would look into her eyes, smell her perfume. She would always repeat the question back to us to make sure she understood it. She made us feel important. We had something important to ask, something worth bending down and listening to. Aunt Lois gave us self-worth.

2. *Treat people as assets.* I learned this truth from my husband's office manager. A parent of four, Carol is a terrific mom. Her family has great mutual respect and love. One day I asked how she achieved it. Carol said that when she and her husband divorced, she realized she would be raising her children alone. Suddenly she needed them as much as they needed her. They learned to rely on one another. "My children are my best friends, my strongest assets," she said.

The best thing we can do for people — child, friend, co-worker or spouse — is to treat them not as liabilities but as assets. I used to rush to the phone before my children could answer it, fearful they'd say the "wrong" thing. Now, I don't care if it's the

White House calling. My best work is in those three faces. They are capable, bright people. Assets. I'm proud of them.

3. *Remember, we are all God's children.* Fran, a former neighbor of mine, is the mother of six. Her children all had natural self-confidence. They were achievers, but weren't obnoxious about it. When I asked about her children one day, she spoke quietly: "Oh, Debbi, these are not really my children. They are God's. They're just on loan to me. It's a privilege to know them. I see each of them as an important house guest, some influential person in embryo."

What a wonderful way to look at children. What a wonderful way to look at everyone! For, you see, Mother's Day isn't just for mothers. It's for all of us.

I now have Owen's Mother's Day drawing framed and hanging in my laundry room. It is one of my favorite pictures because I realize it was drawn innocently by a little boy who loves his mother — even when her hair is sticking up.

Words of Comfort

*Lord, turn the routines of work
into celebrations of love.*
— AUTHOR UNKNOWN

I DON'T WANT TO BE A MOTHER TODAY

SUE MONK KIDD

A tiny wail pierced the silence of the bedroom. I moved mechanically into the worn-out path from my bed to the nursery like a tired old soldier with battle fatigue. The numbers on the clock glowed green, iridescent and grim. It was 4:02 a.m. . . . Mother's Day.

The cry flung itself furiously into the darkness. It was not her hungry-cry. That one had shattered the night at 2:50. This was the colic-cry . . . the third one tonight. I lifted my three-month-old daughter from her crib and dropped wearily into the rocking chair. She screamed into the crook of my elbow. I rocked back and forth,

70

trying to weave time into something bearable. The creak in the chair groaned heavily. *The sound of motherhood,* I thought glumly. My arm began to throb beneath her as sleep crept slowly into her breathing. I dared not move. Just a few more minutes . . .

"MAMA! I'm thirsty," came a loud invisible voice out of the night. I opened my eyes to an abrupt narrow slit. Three-year-old Bob stood in the doorway like a lost shadow. He stepped closer, clutching a stuffed dinosaur.

"Go to bed, and I'll bring some water in a little while." My whisper had the ragged edge of desperation.

"But I want some water now!" he halfway yelled.

The baby jerked and cranked up her cry.

I could almost hear the gasp down inside my heart. "Now look what you did! You woke the baby. Now go to bed!" I shouted. He didn't. He stood there and added his wail to the baby's. It was too much. My eyes turned away, falling on the green diaper pail. It was full again. At the end of the hall, the den was littered with toys, pacifiers, and broken cookies. Beyond that, baby bottles lined the kitchen counter like a miniature skyline. My small world.

And suddenly in that middle-of-the-night moment, something happened deep inside me. The flame of joy that burns so mysteriously inside each mother's heart simply went out. I sat in the nursery like a snuffed candle and drew the darkness around me. Actually, my despondency had been gathering for weeks. It wasn't the kind of thing I liked to admit, but it was true. Something had gradually gone out of my mothering . . . the sparkle, the eagerness, the delight. It had all been swallowed up by an ocean of frustrations and demands. Oh, I loved my children. But, lately, caring for them had become a burden.

The cries raged. "Lord, I know it's Mother's Day," I whispered, near tears myself. "But I don't want to be a mother today. I'm sick of it."

The terrible honesty of my words startled me. How could I say that! How could I feel this way! I wondered if all mothers sometimes despaired of being mothers. Or was it only me?

My husband waded into the shrieking darkness, rubbing his eyes as if he'd wakened into a real live nightmare. "What's going on?" he said.

"I'm thirsty and she don't love me," cried Bob.

The baby squalled, her red face bobbing against my shoulder like a furious woodpecker.

"Here, give the children to me," he said, bravely. "You go to bed."

"They're all yours," I said, thrusting Ann into his arms.

I fell into bed, despising the way I felt. "Oh, Lord, help me," I prayed as I drifted over the edges of sleep. "Help me find some joy again."

I woke to the inevitable wail. My eyes focused on the window where the first sliver of daylight hemmed the curtain with a silver ribbon. The same sense of despondency filled my chest. I rose, dreading the day. I dreaded preparing the children for church . . . the bathing, feeding, dressing, redressing. Every task was like a heavy gray bead on a chain around my neck.

On the drive home from church, Bob's voice floated over the front seat. "We talked about mothers in Sunday school."

"Oh, really," I muttered.

"My teacher said I made you a mother when I was borned."

"It's born. Not borned," I corrected.

"Tell me the story of when I was borned — I mean born."

73

I glanced around at him, getting a whiff of the carnations pinned at my shoulder. His face was poked out with curiosity. "Not now," I said, looking away.

By mid-afternoon the sky was charcoal gray. A slow drizzle of rain washed the den windows. In a rare moment of quiet, I stood at the solemn panes, my depression deepening.

"Mama, *now* will you tell me the story of when I was born?"

I sighed and dropped onto the sofa. He climbed beside me, waiting.

"It was late one night," I began reluctantly. "Daddy and I had waited and waited for you. We thought you never would get here. But finally you decided to come. Daddy drove me to the hospital." I paused, my heart not in the telling.

"Then I was born?" he urged me on.

"Yes. The first time I saw you, you had all your fingers in your mouth making silly noises."

He giggled. "Like this?" He stuck four fingers in his mouth and snorted.

I managed a smile.

"Did you hold me?"

"Yes, we had a long visit that night," I said. "You were wrapped in a blanket, and your hair was combed up into a curl like the top of an ice cream cone."

I could almost see the hair, the small face. It seemed like yesterday.

Outside, lightning splintered the grayness, and inside, Bob's eyes were wide and blue. I looked at the shifting streams on the window and wondered why motherhood could not have remained as fresh and golden as those first moments.

The story seemed ended. But suddenly, a small forgotten piece of it came back to me, almost as if someone had shone a light into a dark place in my memory. "I nearly forgot," I said. "There was a card tucked in your blanket that night. A card from the hospital."

"What did it say?" Bob asked. I squinted my eyes, unable to recall exactly. Suddenly I was searching our shelves, digging out his baby book.

Dust sealed the pages with neglect. Bob hung over my shoulder, his eyes sparkling with mystery as I ruffled through the yellowed memories.

I found the card in the back of the book. Across the front, it was personalized with a slightly faded, slightly smudged inkblot of his hand. Five newly born fingers and one incredibly tiny palm. My eyes drifted over the tender little image down to the inscrip-

tion beneath it . . . a simple greeting card
verse:

"Make the most of every day
For time does not stand still.
One day this hand will wave good-bye
While crossing life's brave hill."

The room grew quiet. Rain trickled on
the panes. Bob took the card; his fingertips
moved in silent wonder along the edge of
the handprint. I watched, my throat feeling
tight. How big his hands had become. And
so quickly. His fingers were long and
skinny next to the little image — his palm
a baseball glove in comparison. And suddenly, his hands holding the tiny inkblot
became a living picture of time moving, of
life flowing swiftly and silently through its
passages. It was a picture of how precious
and fleeting each moment with my children really was.

As Bob clung to the little card, the words
it bore touched me as if they had a secret
magic all their own. There was a truth in
them of immeasurable value, and I could
not resist it. *Make the most of every day.*
Time does not stand still.

It seemed strange how a few lines from
an old verse had returned just when I

needed them. Lines that had somehow made everything clear again and put my problems in their place. *Of course motherhood has frustrations and demands,* I thought. *Every worthwhile thing does. Why not accept them instead of dwell on them? The important thing is to delight in my children now . . . now, before these moments too become yellowed memories.*

With a suddenness that startled us both, I drew Bob to me and hugged him tightly, my heart catching as that fragile flame seemed to ignite again.

"You're going to pop me, Mama," he said, laughing. But I held on. And with his warm little body curved against mine, I looked down at the card, which had tumbled to the floor, and smiled. For I was quite sure this handprint, with its ancient wisdom for mothers printed beneath, was in truth a Mother's Day card . . . one sent specially by God.

The service we render others is the rent
we pay for our room on earth.
— WILFRED GRENFELL

YOU'RE NOT ALONE
MARION BOND WEST

Sometimes young mothers of twins telephone me just to talk. They've read my book about my own twins and sometimes when I answer the phone the only thing I hear at first is sobbing.

I've learned to just wait. As expected, the words come tumbling out between sobs and a good nose blowing. "It's hard work and no fun. No one ever told me how difficult it is to be the mother of twins."

Then I give my little speech. "It's still hard even though they're sixteen now. But I'll tell you a secret. Motherhood isn't easy, period. Before we bring our babies home, the hospital should print on their bracelets: 'Watch out. It won't be easy. But hang in there. It's worth it.' "

"Thank you, thank you," the mothers invariably say. "I thought I was the only mother who didn't like her children every day."

"Well," I reply, "you're certainly not alone. Now, how about trying to help some other mother? One will surely cross your path. Don't be afraid to tell her that some days you just blow it and that you feel like running away from time to time."

Is there someone you can comfort today with the wisdom you've gained through trials of your own?

To be trusted is a greater
compliment than to be loved.
— GEORGE MACDONALD

REMEMBER THE JOY
MARION BOND WEST

I missed my family when I remarried and moved to Oklahoma. It was always a joy to return to Georgia, which my husband and I did often. One day, while back in Georgia, my daughter Julie asked me to pick up four-year-old Katie at kindergarten. Sitting in the long line of cars waiting for my turn to drive by the school door, I recalled the countless times I had done the same thing for my four children.

Katie bounded out to the car, delighted to see me, and we drove off. I had to stop by the drugstore, and as Katie and I got out of the car, she immediately put her hand into mine. She seemed to do it without thinking or making a big deal of it. I'd forgotten what a wondrous thing it is to have a small, trusting hand thrust into your own. As we left the drugstore, once again her hand found mine. No words. Not even a glance. Just her hand securely nestled in mine.

Driving home I thought about the incident. Why, God must feel exactly as I had! What joy He must experience when with complete trust and without fanfare we simply slip our hand into His and walk alongside Him quietly and with absolute faith. It's a joy I want to extend this very day.

*This is the day which
the Lord has made.*
— Psalm 118:24

French Toast Morning
Linda Ching Sledge

It's Saturday morning. I am in my kitchen listening to the coffeemaker bubble and hiss, and the refrigerator whine. In a few minutes, three alarm clocks will buzz and my menfolk will tumble out of bed clamoring for breakfast. Another busy day will begin.

Every day is busy for a working mother. Sometimes I feel like a computer on overload, crammed full of the data of four lives: nursery school projects; homework schedules; the telephone numbers of three good friends willing to watch sick kids at a moment's notice.

I am so used to moving at top speed that it is hard to wind down and rest. Sometimes I resent the demands and the overload. Sometimes I'm angry. Sometimes sad, because I don't feel appreciated.

Yet I know that, alone and idle, I am empty.

The coffeemaker gives one last groan. The thick brown drops fall slower and slower. The refrigerator clanks into silence. I can almost hear the mist caught in the branches of the silver beech tree. Suddenly, You are with me, nearer than my breathing, closer than my beating heart.

Three pairs of feet come clomping downstairs. Three voices sing out to me. I get the skillet and pour myself some coffee. It feels like a French toast morning.

And thou shalt be secure . . .
— JOB 11:18

DO SOMETHING NICE FOR YOURSELF
TERRY HELWIG

My daughter Mandy's glassy eyes and red nose affirmed she wasn't feeling well. "I hurt all over," she sighed. I fluffed her pillow, gave her some medicine, and tucked her in bed.

"How about some chicken noodle soup?" I asked. She smiled and nodded her approval. Chicken noodle soup was her favorite.

A few minutes later, sitting up in bed, she was slurping away. In between one spoonful, she paused, looked my way and said enthusiastically, "You're the best mom in the whole universe."

I squeezed her hand, thankful she felt loved. I remembered when I was a little girl and my mom used to bring me hot tea and toast (my favorite).

As an adult, I often forget that part of me still yearns to be nurtured every now and then. But thanks to a friend's suggestion, I am now doing special little things for myself that evoke warm, secure feelings. Sometimes I light a candle while I write letters. Other times I play my favorite tape, buy myself a rose, or take a walk in the woods — even if my work isn't done.

I'm discovering, like my daughter, that nurturing feels very good. And more likely than not, after I've done something nice for myself, I feel like hugging God and saying with childish enthusiasm, "You're the best God in the whole universe!"

They [older women] can teach
the young women . . .
— TITUS 2:4

LET OTHERS HELP
BONNIE WHEELER

"Lord, forgive me. I was a terrible mother today . . ." I started crying before I could pray any further. I had begun the summer with all the enthusiastic plans an energetic young mother could dream up. But by the end of August, all that was left were three squabbling kids and their frazzled mother. And now here I was embarrassing myself by breaking down at my women's prayer meeting.

Another young mother followed, "Oh, Lord, I also was so short-tempered with my little Jeannie tonight." Karen started weeping along with me.

Then Betty, a woman in her late forties, started praying for us both. She well remembered those long end-of-summer days with small kids. "Lord, help Bonnie and Karen," Betty began. "Help them to be the godly mothers You want them to be. Comfort them in their need. And, Lord, help them to forgive themselves."

I was buoyed by the prayers and offers of help from the others. Before summer ended, the kids and I returned to the park and the zoo; my husband and I found time together, too. I discovered I didn't have to do it alone.

Are you shouldering a burden or responsibility that is crushing you? Listen to one who foolishly tried to do it alone. Turn to others — a spouse, a friend, a small support group. Let the understanding of others heal you, let their prayers guide you, and by all means say "Yes!" to their offers of help.

Not in the achievement,
but in the endurance of the human soul
does it show . . . its alliance with
the infinite God.
— EDWIN HUBBEL CHAPIN

LOOK WITH GOD'S EYES

BONNIE WHEELER

Graduation Day. My youngest daughter Becki is standing in front of the full-length mirror with me behind her. We both stare into it as I adjust her collar, secure her cap, drape the stole around her neck that signifies her high grade point average, attach the gold pin for lifetime membership in the state honor society, and hang a bronze medallion around her neck that shows she's graduating *cum laude.*

Suddenly, the image of my daughter standing proudly in her cap and gown is replaced with the image of a frightened three-year-old in a wheelchair. I see a parade of doctors declaring, "She has cerebral palsy! She'll never walk!" Meanwhile, a host of social workers are busily stamping "Unadoptable!" across her files. But God gave us a glimpse of how He saw Becki with her loving demeanor and joyful giggle, and He gave us the grace to see past those outward appearances. Becki joined our family.

Looking back, I remember years filled with surgeries, therapy, and lots of hard work and determination from Becki. And now on this day, Becki isn't just graduating. She's *walking* down the aisle to receive her diploma.

Even in the face of what seems to be sorrow and trouble, God blesses us only with good. The secret is in looking with the eyes of the Lord.

We are always in the forge,
or on the anvil; by trials God
is shaping us for higher things.
— HENRY WARD BEECHER

BLACKBERRY SEASONS
MARY LOU CARNEY

When I was a child, spring seemed to take forever in coming. As soon as the April sun began warming the creek, I'd want to go barefoot. Grandma would shake her head "no." Then mild May days would coax blooms from marsh marigolds and trillium. "It's summer!" I'd laugh, tossing my warm sweaters up into the top of the closet. "We ain't had blackberry winter yet," Grandma would say with conviction.

"Blackberry winter" — that's what my grandmother called that final cold snap in May, when blackberries began to ripen. And she was always right. Before the month was over, I'd have to retrieve a sweater for a few days.

Now that I'm an adult, I've noticed "blackberry winters" in other areas of my life, too. I save for a vacation, but have to spend the money on a new washer. My "meaningful relationship" with my two teenagers is occasionally splintered. Sometimes I'm tempted to give up. I feel things will never get better.

That's when I think of Grandma, sitting in her rocker, her hands stitching quilting pieces. "It'll never get warm!" I used to whine.

" 'Course it will," she'd laugh. "Blackberry winter is a short season, child."

And that's the way I try to think of my setbacks, too. Inevitable. Short-lived. As natural as the seasons, the "blackberry seasons" of life.

Trouble knocked at the door,
but hearing a laugh within,
it hurried away.
— BENJAMIN FRANKLIN

TO BE BLUNT
LINDA NEUKRUG

Although my Grandma Rae was house-bound because of severe arthritis, she never let it get her down. She was well-read, informed on news events, and through TV was up on all the latest trends. Visitors dropped by daily, myself included. One time a friend came to spend an hour cheering up Grandma. But it seemed that all she wanted to do was complain — about the weather, about a lazy husband, about a son who didn't visit often, about . . .

Grandma listened patiently, but when the woman began listing *Grandma's* troubles ("Oh, you poor dear, you can't walk"), Grandma put a stop to that right away. "I make it a point," she said firmly, "to forget

92

my troubles as easily as most folks forget their blessings."

I remember being shocked at Grandma's blunt words and wondering how her friend would take them. But after a short pause, the woman laughed and began talking about the pleasure she got from her gardening and other hobbies!

I've always remembered these words. They come to me whenever I'm tempted to let my troubles cloud out a clear and sunny day.

When a man has no strength,
if he leans on God,
he becomes powerful.
— Dwight Lyman Moody

Ready to Shine!
Mary Lou Carney

"Hand me the lamp, young'un," Grandma said, reaching for the kerosene jug on the floor of the pantry.

I lifted the old lamp from its place on the shelf. Carefully Grandma removed the glass globe, trimmed the wick, and began pouring kerosene into the base. "Got to keep her filled — just in case this newfangled stuff gives out," she'd say, waving at the light bulb overhead.

Often that "new stuff" did give out. That's when Grandma would set that kerosene lamp in the center of the kitchen table, where its rays helped push back the darkness. And her satisfied smile was visible even in the dim light.

94

Sometimes I feel like I'm running out of "oil": I volunteer for one too many committees; I neglect reading my Bible; I convince myself that hot dogs really are nutritious. But soon I find I'm irritable, tired, and discouraged. I snap at the kids, grumble when my husband is late for dinner. I am less creative and more sarcastic. That's when I seem to hear Grandma saying, "Got to keep her filled." So I take time for a long walk in the woods or a leisurely bubble bath. I thumb through a magazine, treat myself to Mexican food, play checkers with my son. I read the Gospels. I turn my prayers into praises. And, like Grandma's kerosene lamp, I soon find I'm "filled up" and ready to shine!

*Motherhood is, after all,
woman's great and incomparable work.*
— EDWARD CARPENTER

MOM'S THE ONE
DEBORAH SHOUSE

"Mom!" a girlish voice calls out in a busy store. I turn toward it. So do several other women. It doesn't matter that I'm in the store alone or that my two daughters are much older than this helpless little voice. When I hear "Mom!" I am poised for action, ready for rescue. Sure, they all say "Dada" first, but we women know it's just because their tiny mouths can't yet reach the round wonder of the word *Mom*. In those three letters, so much is said. Like Esperanto, *Mom* holds universal meaning.

"Mom . . . *Mom*." The sound is a vapor trail through my sleep. Jessica has dropped her teddy bear; her blanket is out of reach. I stumble into her room, tuck her stuffed bear in beside her, smooth her blanket over her, lean into the crib, kiss her, and whisper my love. Eyes closed, I wander back to bed. I don't need to turn on lights — I know the way too well.

"Mom!" The word stabs at me even after I have driven away from the city's finest day-care center. All the teachers have college degrees and are certified in kindness. The rooms are bright, the children diverse, the groups small, and the educational content stimulating. Yet as I walk out of the place, something in my heart cries out, wailing.

Once in my office, I call, expecting to hear her screams in the background. "Oh, Jessica stopped crying the moment you left," the teacher assures me.

Mom is defined in the dictionary as "a female parent." But through the years my children — Jessica, the firstborn, and Sarah, who arrived four years later — have used the word to mean much more.

At age four, when Sarah cries, "Maaawwm!" I know she has misbuttoned her shirt or jammed her zipper.

Jessica, at seven, shrieks "Mo-hom" in an accusatory tone. She can't find a matching sock. Her tone changes as she gets older. She learns to lilt the word, to speak it sweetly: will I please iron her yellow dress?

Sarah, at thirteen, spits out her "Moms." On a morning when she's already late for school, "Mom!" means "I am desperate for new clothes. I can't believe I've existed in these rags."

Jessica, at the age when she starts driving to school, still "Moms" when her clothes are dirty or wrinkled or boring — only now "Mom" translates to "May I *please* borrow your new silk blouse?"

"Mom?" Sarah is almost seventeen and rarely knocks on my door in the morning anymore. Yet I recognize the vulnerability in her voice.

"Do you want help typing your paper?" I ask her, sleep-blurred.

She nods, then bursts into tears. "John's mad at me, and I don't know why. He won't talk to me. . . ."

I put my arm around her. I make tea, hand her a box of tissues, and wait for her to talk. Part of me wants to shield my child from the cruel beasts who make her weep so, yet another part of me knows she gains strength from the struggle.

"Mom, what should I do?"

Her plea burrows into my heart like an arrow. I wish the answer were still simple. I wish I could find the sock, lend the blouse, and end up being the hero.

But I've got problems of my own just now. I'm exhausted. I feel the drain of being responsible for myself and my daughters. I am tired of being a grown-up. I talk to my friends and they empathize. I talk to my brother and he problem-solves. I need more.

So I dial the familiar number I once called from college, then from my trailer in Alabama, from the duplex in Germany, and from a series of homes throughout the Midwest.

"Hello?" The voice is crackly, uncertain. It has lived through so much already that it's leery of another blow.

"Mom?" I say.

"Honey, are you all right?" my mother asks.

Somehow, that is everything I want to hear.

*God always gives his very best to those
who leave the choice with him.*
— JAMES HUDSON TAYLOR

I CHOOSED YOU

MARJORIE HOLMES

It's no secret that I didn't want my fourth child. I was in tears when our family doctor confirmed it. "But I already *have* three children — one of them ready for college. I thought I'd finally have more time for other things I enjoy!"

"Please don't take it like that," he tried to comfort me. "I'm sure this child will be a great blessing to you."

Oh, he says that to all his patients, I thought. *He's just being kind.* But Melanie was a joy and special treasure to all of us from the moment she arrived. And as she grew older, she grew in grace, delight, and beauty, with a wisdom that at times astonished me. Best of all, she loved the Lord.

I remember a time when she was barely

100

five years old. We were walking past a church, and as she danced along beside me she was chanting a little made-up song: "Oh, oh, oh, I think you are the nicest mommy in the world. Oh, oh, oh, I love you, and you know why? When I was a baby angel in heaven God asked me: 'Look down and see which mother do you choose?' and I said, 'Eenie, meenie, mineymo, catch a mommy by the toe. If she hollers let her go.' *But I choosed you!*"

It seemed funny at the time; only later did I feel its deeper significance. And even today I sometimes wonder: in the mysteries of creation, isn't it possible there are little souls somewhere just waiting to be born? Perhaps even choosing the parents God wants them to have?

Perhaps someone reading this today has a new life stirring within her. Unexpected, and yes, unwelcome. If you are such a someone, please remember this true story. Such a child can be a tremendous joy and comfort — beyond your wildest dreams. Perhaps there is a tiny angel somewhere who "choosed you" because God wanted it to, a child who will fill a special need in your life as it develops into a beautiful life of its own.

Accept this for the precious gift it is, and be thankful.

A grateful thought toward heaven
is of itself a prayer.
— GOTTHOLD EPHRAIM LESSING

GRATITUDE FOR ANSWERED PRAYERS
GAIL GRENIER SWEET

The warming waters poured over my head and body. Lifting my face, I closed my eyes. "Dear God, please send me a little being who needs my love. I beg this of you. I will be a good mother." It was March of 1984, and there I was praying in the manner of the ancients — arms extended. Never before had I prayed that way, yet for the first time it seemed the natural thing to do, and I did so without thinking. I was in the shower, my favorite praying place. I imagined, as always, that the water was the white light of God, surrounding me with radiance. . . .

On December 2, 1984, our little Anna Rose joined us in this world. She has been beauty and joy — and health — since the first day of her life . . . More than ever before, I am amazed at the miracle of life. I was full of wonder when my sons were born, but it seems that now I am even more humbled by all the gifts I've received. Maybe it's because I'm older and take things less for granted. Every day I marvel at the fact that Anna Rose is here, that she's healthy, and that she can take nourishment from my body.

Once I heard the story of an old Buddhist who was asked what the best prayer was. The old man said, "There is only one proper prayer. And it is this: THANK YOU." Thank you, dear God.

The Best Example

Faith never knows where it is being led,
but it loves and knows
the one who is leading.
— OSWALD CHAMBERS

MAMA AND THE ENCYCLOPEDIAS
JOYCE REAGIN

One day after school there was a knock at our door. Mama opened it. A lady selling encyclopedias stood there. "Come on in!" Mama said.

She knew how much I wanted a set, but I knew we didn't have the money. Still, Mama depended on the Lord for everything — even encyclopedias. In fact, she had cleared and dusted a shelf in the living room to make room for the new books. "They're at the top of my prayer list," she told me. That was Mama for you!

"Do sit down," Mama said to the saleslady. Soon the two were chatting like old friends. Then Mama showed me the handsome sample volumes. I fell in love with the white, leather-bound books.

"I can manage the monthly payments," Mama said, "but it's the money I have to give you now that I'd have trouble scraping together." The encyclopedia lady frowned.

"I understand," she told Mama. "I guess we can't always have the things we want." She began picking up her samples. "For instance, there was this one-of-a-kind pair of shoes I had been admiring, but I kept putting off buying them. When I finally got around to it, they were gone — bought on sale for next to nothing! I could've died. Some lucky shopper got a real bargain."

Suddenly Mama smiled. She excused herself from the room and returned with a pair of brand-new shoes.

"Those arc the ones!" the lady gasped.

"Try them on," Mama insisted.

They were a perfect fit. "Would you consider the shoes as the down payment for the encyclopedias?" Mama asked.

Two weeks later I was arranging our shiny new encyclopedias on the dust-free shelf. I knew those books would teach me a lot. But they could never teach me as much as Mama did about faith.

To be honest as this world goes, is to be one man picked out of a thousand.
— WILLIAM SHAKESPEARE

LET'S BE HONEST
CAROL KNAPP

Brenda is thirteen. "Frienda Brenda," I call her. She's a blond dynamo full of big plans and ideas, not all of which fly. Take last summer: She figured she'd save half-price on admission to the Alaska State Fair by passing herself off as twelve. Her plan was tempting, I'll admit — our fun money was limited — but the *Wrong Way* warning flashed in my mind and I firmly told her, "No."

A month later, Brenda sat in English class and cheated on a vocabulary test by furtively looking up a definition. All weekend it bothered her. On Monday, she confessed to the teacher. The first I knew of it was the paper she handed me marked with a glaring red F, softened by the instructor's scribbled, "Thanks for being honest."

Honesty costs . . . but it buys a clear conscience. And honesty is hereditary — we parents tend to pass it on to our kids! That *Wrong Way* signal I caught back at the state fair is the same one that kept Brenda truthful — alone and on her own — in the classroom.

Do we want teens who live with integrity? Then you and I must first choose to walk straight ourselves. It's God's High Way and it works . . . honest!

*All the troubles of life come upon us
because we refuse to sit quietly for a while
each day in our room.*
— BLAISE PASCAL

MOTHER'S LESSON
RICK HAMLIN

It was one of Mother's rules. Every day, when we were little, she made us stay in our rooms, by ourselves, for about twenty minutes. "I needed to get you out of my hair," she later explained. Actually, she was following the advice of some long-forgotten child psychologist she had read in a magazine. The point was that children should learn to entertain themselves. They should know the pleasures of being alone.

I can still recall those quiet afternoons when I watched the eucalyptus trees outside my window quaking in the breeze. I can remember seeing the ocean from a rented beach house, sunlight scattered on the sea like glitter spilled from a bottle. I

110

can recall quiet times of creating cartoons out of cracks on my bedroom ceiling and making pictures out of the long shadows cast on my linoleum floor. I learned to enjoy being alone.

I've heard it said that we need to be quiet for God to speak to us — we need to be empty of the projects, schemes, worries, and doubts that get in the way of His working through us. When Jesus needed to be closer to God, He always sought some time alone. When I feel far from God, I try to do the same . . . putting into practice a lesson my mother taught long ago.

*Music exalts each joy, allays each grief,
expels disease, softens every pain.*
— JOHN ARMSTRONG

SONG ACROSS THE YEARS
LOUISE A. DRIVER

Mom is far from beautiful — "nice looking" probably describes her better. Her hair is graying, and the wrinkles in her hands are more distinct, which is not surprising because Mom has worked hard all her life.

When we kids were growing up, we lived in the tiny community of Minong, Wisconsin. Dad and Mom ran a live-bait stand for a living. Because most of the bait we sold was bought by tourists during the summer months, winters were sometimes hard, but Mom was always cheerful.

Mom raised a vegetable garden. Each summer she canned over seventy-five quarts of string beans, besides all the other vegetables, "to make ends meet," Mom always said. Mom used to sit on our porch and snap the beans and sing. I never thought much about her singing. It was just what you heard when you opened the door, or while you watched her washing the dishes.

One day the singing stopped. I was too young to remember an exact day. But all at once I realized Mom wasn't singing any more. She looked tense and tired. Waking up one night and hearing her crying, I knew what was happening. The following day we were told. Our parents' marriage was ending — in divorce.

The day came in June. The truck loaded all our belongings and left Dad's behind. We moved to Rice Lake, where my mom could find work.

She must have been very unhappy and very scared, all alone, with two young children still at home to support. But she just told my brother and me that she loved us and that somehow things would turn out all right.

Even though she worked many long hours, Mom found time to remember the little things. She remembered Easter baskets and orange birthday cakes with blue frosting and animal candleholders and even our old plastic Christmas stockings. Mom probably could have made a lot of new friends in Rice Lake, but we kept her too busy to try.

Mom could never hate. She tried to explain why she thought the divorce had happened and taught us to love Dad. She never would let us criticize or blame him.

Mom helped me through the growing-up years. She rode around and around the block with me when I was learning to drive. She stood up proudly at my honors banquet and graduation from high school. She was always there.

I remember one trying period during those high school years. I was very discouraged. I finally told Mom I had lost God. I explained how he seemed so far away and unreachable that I'd stopped praying to him.

"Are you really looking for him," Mom said, "or are you waiting for him to run to you? For if you are, he has already run. Turn around and meet him halfway." I knew Mom was right. I started to pray again, and as I prayed, my faith returned.

Several years later, I married David Driver. It wasn't an easy wedding for Mom. She didn't want Dad to walk me down the aisle. She said that she felt he had lost his right to do that. I thought she was wrong, and we talked a lot about it. Finally one night as we lay talking in our shared bedroom, Mom settled it. She said she had prayed and the answer seemed to say, "Anne, look at Louise and forget about Merril." After the wedding, Mom told me she had done just that, and it worked. Mom has never interfered in our marriage.

Not long ago, as I stood one night in the bedroom of our two small children and looked from bed to crib, I suddenly found myself praying: "Dear Lord, let my children love and respect me as I love and respect Mom. Help me, Lord, to teach them the things that I have been taught: that there is always a loving mother to call on when everything else seems impossible and that you are always near to watch. Amen."

The next time I saw Mom I told her about that prayer. She didn't say anything. But when we went to Mom's for supper a few nights later and opened the door, you know what I heard? I heard Mom singing.

After all those years, Mom was singing.

Don't pray when you feel like it. Have an
appointment with the Lord and keep it.
A man is powerful on his knees.
— CORRIE TEN BOOM

MOMMY PRAYING
LINDA J. BURBA

I could tell from the start that this day would
be no exception. Three-year-old Matthew
climbed into bed with me, lay there quietly
for no more than two minutes, with his ice-
cold feet robbing warmth from my legs, and
then began squirming.

"Let's wake up, Mom. I want breakfast."
I grunted assent, though my eyelids were
still heavy with sleep, and my head bur-
rowed into the pillow a bit deeper. When
the whining picked up in intensity, I knew
Matt would soon have his twin brother,
Michael, and baby Mark aroused. I got out
of bed.

So the morning started. After breakfast,
I gave Mark his bath while Matt and Mike

pulled all their toys out on the living-room floor. Then they ransacked three drawers in their bedroom, fought over who got to wear the new yellow socks, and came out crying because, alas, this was a washday and favorite clothes were still in the laundry. I pulled out some alternative shirts and pants and tried to convince the twins that these would do.

Soon Mark began rubbing his eyes and fussing a little. It was time for his morning nap. Another diaper change, and he was down in his crib for the time being.

The twins by now were all dressed — underpants on backwards on Matt, shirt on backwards on Mike, but nevertheless dressed. We sat on the couch and read a children's story, knelt down to pray before the day's play, and they were off.

This would be one of the two quiet times of the day. I had learned early in my Christian life, long before we had children, that my spiritual well-being is dependent on daily communion with God. But finding a time of quiet was another question. With three small boys, there never seemed enough chance to concentrate on "effective, fervent prayer," eyes closed and shutting out the world. After putting a load of wash in the machine, making beds, and straightening the house a little, there was barely time for the reading part of my devotions. *I'll pray during their afternoon naps,* my mind noted.

I sat down with the Bible at the kitchen table where I could see the front yard. I'd been reading through the psalms, noticing what distinct mood changes David went through. I think David must have understood mothers.

Shortly, Matt came running in. "Mom, Laura and Jennifer say I'm 'icky'," he complained. "They hate boys." I told him to ignore them. He didn't know what "ignore" meant, but it seemed to satisfy him that he had tattled. He ran back out.

I read a few more verses.

Matt sauntered back. "I need a rag."

"What for?"

"To wash the porch!" (Said in an isn't-it-obvious tone.)

Rather than argue, I got him a rag. I vaguely wondered where he would get the water, but decided I would solve that problem if it arose. Right now I was *trying* to have my devotions.

Mike came to the window, walking stiff-legged as if he'd delayed a certain duty too long. That was not the problem, I soon found out. "Mom, Matt wetted me with the hose." I yelled at Matt to turn off that hose, and I got Mike some dry clothes.

I read a few more verses. The next interruption in my reading was Mike's, too. "Can I go bare feet like Matthew Wing?"

"Of course," I responded without enthusiasm. "Put your shoes in the house so the puppy won't carry them away."

"Can't I just put them on the picnic table?" Always an alternative plan!

"Sure." And I got through a few more verses.

Matt came around. "Mom, can I take off my shoes like Mike?"

"Okay. Put your shoes on the picnic table so Clipper won't carry them off."

"I thought we're s'posed to put our shoes in the house."

"Either place is all right today." I was trying to read.

Finally, they went off to play at their friend's house. Mark awakened as I finished the psalm I was reading. Its praise section was uplifting, and for a moment I reflected on the sentiments Paul expresses in another part of the Bible: "In whatsoever state I am, therewith to be content" (Phil. 4:11).

I hummed a tune as I resumed my tasks, remembering the day's beginning when I had knelt beside my bed for a few moments of prayer. I'd looked up and seen Matt's pleased smile as he knelt directly across from me, hands folded, listening. He had said, "I prayed to Jesus, too, Mom. And I thanked him for my mommy praying here right now."

My moments with God's word lift me. The prayers encourage me. And little lives are watching, listening, and learning from my daily example.

When the boys are grown up, they won't remember the interruptions. But I hope they will remember seeing Mom read her Bible and hearing Mom pray.

Love is an Art,
and the greatest of the Arts.
— EDWARD CARPENTER

LOVE IN A CREAM-COLORED DRESS
DIANE SKINNER

Love comes in many ways; it is hidden in mystical sizes, shapes, and colors. One April it came to me wrapped in creamy white.

It all began three weeks before Mom's birthday. I spent hours gathering thoughts for just the right gift. Being an independent eight-year-old, I refused to settle for a gift bought by Dad. I thumbed through a catalog as I mulled over choices. A fantastic idea overwhelmed me. This year Mom would have the best present ever! I'd give her a cream-colored dress which Grandma and I would make.

The next morning I revealed my secret plan to Gram and enlisted her aid. To-

121

gether we drove to town, embarking on our great adventure. To my amazement, I found gorgeous cream-colored fabric in the very first store. It was as beautiful as I had visualized. I smiled with delight as I pictured the dress of Mom's dreams.

The following days after school and on Saturdays, I crept over to Gram's. I insisted on supervising the dress construction; after all, it was my idea! To make matters better, Gram had carefully chosen the pattern from her collection, one of Mom's favorites that had been used before during her school days.

After three tedious weeks of cutting and sewing, the garment was complete. Gram included real cloth-covered buttons and a belt. Was I excited!

The day of Mom's birthday arrived. I just knew she would think mine the best gift of all. Impetuously I laid it on top of all her gifts.

After blowing out the candles and slowly finishing the last bite of her cake, Mom was at last ready to open gifts. I could hardly stand the suspense. Reaching for my present first, she placed it in her lap. Slowly she removed the shiny bow from the striped paper. Gingerly Mom lifted the cream-colored dress from the white tissue lining. She appeared to be dazed. With misty eyes she then turned and looked at me, a tender smile upon her face. Watching her, my heart danced with delight, sensing her love and approval.

I looked forward to each occasion when Mom would wear her special dress. My greatest anticipation was the church mother-daughter luncheon. The day of the luncheon, I skipped to Mom's room. There on her bed lay a blue suit — in place of the dress! Mentioning that her new shoes would not match the dress, she said she'd wear her new suit. Seeing my tears spill down, however, she quietly rehung her suit.

With Mom's passing I discovered these facts. Not only did she dislike the color cream, but she had quietly vowed never again to wear a homemade dress. Her teenage years were during the Depression when money was scarce and clothing was handmade. Ever since, she had filled her closet with store-bought clothing.

Today I can see what real love means and what love meant to Mom. To her it meant wearing a dress she didn't like because she loved me. Yes, Mother not only taught me love, but lived it by wearing her special dress.

*Love puts the fun in together . . . the sad
in apart . . . the hope in tomorrow . . .
the joy in a heart.*
— AUTHOR UNKNOWN

LOVE WILL
KEEP US CLOSE
FRANCES LIMING

My mother used to tell me about the time
when I was five years old and overheard a
friend tell her, "My, your Frances is getting
big. Soon she'll be leaving you and going to
school." That night my mother heard me
praying, "You can do it, Jesus. I know you
can." When my mother questioned me, I explained, "I just asked Jesus to keep me small
enough so I'll never have to leave you."

"But Jesus wants you to grow tall and go
to school," my mother told me. "Love will
keep us close, no matter how far apart we
are."

Obviously my prayers weren't answered

by keeping me physically small. I went to school, married, and had a child of my own. But my prayers were answered in the very close relationship I always had with my mother.

Even so, I never fully understood what she told me until my son Steve volunteered for Army service and left for training camp. At first I missed him dreadfully. Then one day I remembered my mother's "love will keep us close," and I was able to overcome my feelings of aloneness. Though we were separated, love did indeed keep Steve and me close — through mail, telephone, and our concern for each other. As an adult I was able to say, with the same faith as the five-year-old, "You can do it, Jesus."

Though old the thought and oft exprest,
'tis his at last who says it best.
— JAMES RUSSELL LOWELL

A NOTE ON THE KITCHEN TABLE

MARGARET LEV

There isn't a day goes by that I don't think of my mother and her sayings. She had values that she tried to instill in us; she taught us how to treat others, and good manners, table and otherwise.

Today I sometimes wonder if I stressed these values enough in my own children. Much of what I always felt was important seems to have gotten lost in today's society.

I wish I had put a note on my kitchen table for my children to read, and to pass on to the grandchildren. It would contain the teachings that I will always dearly thank my own mother for.

Besides the Golden Rule of treating

others as you wished to be treated yourself, she had such advice as "Don't tarry (hang around) where you aren't welcomed" and "Keep your hands off things that don't belong to you." My children heard these enough times, but I don't believe I ever put it in writing.

My mother had many delightful sayings and I never did know where she got them. Two of my favorites were "Much wants more"(someone who has a lot but is never satisfied) and "Either one would spoil another couple"(said about two "dysfunctional" people who belonged together — though you wonder how they ever managed to find one another!).

*The most rewarding things you do in life
are often the ones that look like they
cannot be done.*
— ARNOLD PALMER

MY MOTHER, HELOISE
PONCÉ HELOISE CRUSE

"Hi, how are you?" My mother used to walk up to people and say that all the time. Then she'd introduce herself, "I'm Heloise. You know, the lady who writes the helpful hints column. I noticed the shine on that table you're polishing (this to a cleaning lady in the lobby of a posh London hotel). Could you please tell me what you're using?"

"Vinegar, madame."

"Vinegar!" exclaimed Mom. "Why, I've never heard. . . ."

Mom chatted with this stranger as though she were a next-door neighbor while, as usual, I nearly died of embarrassment. But it was a great day for vinegar. Vinegar became a favorite household helper in Mom's column.

That was Mother, uninhibited, friendly, and so eager to learn how to make life run smoothly that she'd ask people everywhere — in restaurants, shops, taxis, on the street — their secret cures and shortcuts for mending life's little problems.

"It's the little things that drive you crazy — the broken heel, the stain, the drop. If you take care of the little things, the big things become manageable."

That was her philosophy, and it became her career in 1959 when she marched into the newspaper in Honolulu (where our family was stationed) and offered to write a "Reader's Exchange" column of helpful tips. "I'll do it free for a month," she told the editor.

Mom had never written professionally in her life, but the editor agreed to let her try, and then watched his paper's circulation increase by more than thirty percent during the next three years. He claimed it was mostly due to Mother's column.

I was seven when Mother started it, and I remember our family — Dad, a captain in the Air Force, my older brother, Louis, me, and Mom — sitting at the dinner table discussing tips sent in by readers.

"Here's a letter that says you can shine

silver with toothpaste. Poncé, run, get the toothpaste! Let's see if it works."

It did. And Mom used it in her column.

Another time, she told us, "A lady wrote that she was about to throw away her daughter's old petticoat, one of those stiff net ones that had begun drooping. Instead, she cut it up and used it for scrubbing pots and pans."

We laughed. Scrubbing pots with petticoats! But Mother went right out, bought some nylon net, and scoured all of our pots and pans. "It works!" she told her readers, and that idea became one of the most successful in her column.

I can see Mom now, pounding out tips on her typewriter in her folksy style as though she were writing to a good friend. And her readers *were* good friends. She'd tell me, "Homemakers are the backbone of the country. If life becomes a mess at home, it will fall apart everywhere else."

Mother wrote books; she made public appearances. She did radio and TV shows. She worked as a hospital volunteer. She wrote a song. She even did fine paintings. But, above all, she was a homemaker. Her heart was in the home and with the people who kept it.

She understood the irksome nuisances of

homemakers. (She lived with them, too.) And she was tireless in finding their solutions: "Your cottage cheese going moldy? Store it upside down next time." Mom found solutions for everything from taking off garlic skins to putting on a girdle. She taught me that one of the best solutions in life is persistence.

I remember yelling from the sewing machine one day, "Mom, I can't get this zipper right. It's full of ridges!"

"Poncé," she told me, "you've got to rip it out, honey, and stitch it in again. It will never zip that way."

I put it in again. Nothing but bunches and puckers.

"Dear, that's all wrong. Try it again." *Snip. Snip. Snip. Ch-ch-ch-ch-ch-ch,* I stitched around the zipper. "Ugh! It looks awful, Mom."

"Just rip it out and start over," Mother said.

And I did. Over and over and over. It took me seventeen tries to get that zipper in flat. The rest of the garment was ruined from all of the ripping out. But I knew how to put in a zipper. And you'd better believe, I never forgot!

Mom was like that, persistent, when it came to her relationship with God. She kept her word, just as she did at home and with her readers.

One of her promises is still ongoing, even though Mother died in 1977. It began when I was born. My eyes were so crossed that you could see only the whites. The doctors were doubtful that I'd ever be able to see correctly. Well, Mom wanted me to see. The doctors said it would take five operations to straighten out my eyes, and then they shrugged over the possible outcome. They wouldn't give her much hope.

So Mom said to God, "Please, if you'll cure my Poncé, I'll tithe my income to the blind." The operations worked, and fifteen percent of Mom's income, even from her estate today, has always gone to purchase Braille typewriters for kids who can't afford them.

Always persistent in giving back to God, that was Mom. You see, she wanted her spiritual life to run smoothly, too.

You have to work on the little things — those little spiritual problems inside of you. You iron those out. Then you work on those little messy tasks around the home — those greasy, drippy, dusty, creaky, nagging little frustrations that take away your home's harmony. Day by day, with persistence.

That was Mother's way of making the home. Her way of making it a place of safety, a place of comfort, a place where people could feel joy, peace. A place where each of us could come and know that we belonged, a place where we could be restored and go out to meet the challenges of the day.

Once upon a time, being a homemaker was women's work — proud work. Many people don't feel this way today. With so many women in the work force, being a housekeeper often seems trivial. But I myself believe that we need the homemaker more than ever.

Straightening. Ironing. Mending. Gluing. Polishing. These things go on, day by day. The home is where we start from and come back to, and the homemaker — women, and men, too — remains "the backbone of our country."

Mother understood and loved and honored homemakers; she wanted to make their daily tasks easier; and now, as the "Hints from Heloise" columnist, so do I. I've come to love and revere all those people who are proud to put their energies each day into making the home a glorious place to be.

Being
Strong

I will not leave you comfortless:
I will come to you.
— JOHN 14:18

BUBBLES AND ROSE PETALS

AND THE

SMOOTHNESS OF SATIN

NANCY L. RILEY

"I can't do it," I said softly, then a little louder, "I just can't do it!"

I slumped against the wall of my bedroom and slid down to the floor. Head in hands, I started to cry and mutter. After a few minutes of self-pity, I looked over at my tiny three-month-old son, lying on the floor on a baby blanket.

Already Seth had endured surgery twice — with another operation scheduled before his first birthday. Added to his

struggle to survive was this sad diagnosis
— Down syndrome.

Three weeks after his birth, my husband
and I had taken him to a rehabilitation
center in Fort Collins for an "evaluation."
We were told that we were fortunate to be
so young and full of energy (we are both in
our twenties), and we could be thankful
that we had only one child so far. Raising
him would be a lot of hard work, the evalu-
ating therapy team warned us.

" 'Normal' babies seek out their own
stimulation from the environment," the
therapist told us. Our baby would be pas-
sive and content to lie still in his crib. If we
wanted to enhance his development beyond helplessness, we would have to "stim-
ulate" him.

Somehow, I didn't understand the idea
of "stimulation." I wanted to protect Seth
from life's difficulties. Instead, three times
a week, we visited therapists, who manipulated his slender limbs and coaxed his
toneless muscles to work. Timidly at first, I
attempted to imitate them at home. Gradually it became easier to exercise his legs
and play with his soft hands. But something was missing. I didn't seem to be getting anywhere with this concept of "infant
stimulation."

Now Seth was watching me watch him as I leaned my head against the wall and asked, "Why should I prod and push you until you cry? Why can't I just sit in a cozy rocking chair and hold you tight?"

He just stared back at me curiously, his arms limp at his sides and his legs sprawled uselessly on the blanket. *What is going on in his mind as he stares at me?* I wondered. And suddenly the thought came that Seth must find me a very depressing mother. All I seemed to do was stare at him and wonder what to do with him next. *Is that all he will remember of his childhood?* I wondered. *Heaven forbid!* I squeezed my eyes shut tight and prayed to God that I'd find a way to help my baby.

Well, what about my own childhood? Maybe that would help. What good things could I remember? Treating myself to some reminiscent daydreaming, I started with the "Princess Purple Comforter" dream.

When I was eight, we moved from a small town in Nebraska to a bustling college town in Colorado. My parents divorced shortly after the move. My sister and I lived with our mother in an apartment building that had a storage attic full of padlocked "cribs" for extra belongings, one for each apartment. One afternoon while my mother was at work, I felt particularly lost and sad, so I took the padlock key off its nail and stole away up three flights of stairs to the attic.

It was quiet and tranquil up there; I still remember the musty smell. By the time I had opened the padlock to our crib, I was sweating from nervousness and the stuffy atmosphere. Would I be discovered as I explored this forgotten treasure chest? There wasn't much treasure to look at, mostly just Christmas decorations in boxes. But then I saw it — a dark purple comforter inviting me to slip my hands between its cool, satin folds.

Before long, I was parading between the cribs with the comforter wrapped around my shoulders, trailing behind on the dusty wooden floor. Such a rich, deep purple! Such smooth fabric! For a few minutes, I was a beautiful princess, advancing stately through statue-filled palace gardens, nodding and smiling serenely at my retainers. . . .

After trying to fold the comforter the way I had found it (it kept sliding off the boxes), I padlocked the crib and scurried down the steps before Mom arrived home. But that was just my first visit. I made many more trips up those steps to luxuriate in the comforter's satiny softness.

Now, as I sat with my infant son looking up at me, I smiled at him, remembering the smooth satin comforter and the luxurious feeling it gave me whenever I wrapped myself in it.

"Your skin is that soft, too, Seth," I told him. *Isn't it funny,* I thought, *how a special memory can make a person feel so much better — just the way recalling a certain Bible verse can bring comfort at difficult times.*

One of the worst times in my life had been when my father died a year before Seth was born. I recalled standing in the cemetery on a cold January afternoon. While the wind whipped my skirt around and turned up my collar, I read the message on a grave marker: "I will not leave you comfortless; I will come to you" (John 14:18). And at that moment the pleasant memories of my father came rushing back and made me feel so good that I found myself smiling.

That did it for me in my dilemma with Seth. I decided to make certain that our son would have plenty of memories of God's Word, and plenty of memories of good things in life to see him through the rough days ahead.

"Let's see now . . . what will your memories be?" I asked him. He only blinked his eyes. I smiled and glanced at a shiny blue bed cover on the floor of my closet. It was a satin comforter. I had forgotten we had one. Without hesitation, I slipped it out and pulled it over to where Seth was lying. Tenderly, I placed him in the center of the folded comforter. His eyes grew very large and he stiffened for a moment. Then he slowly turned his head to the side and moved his arm up and down, sliding it gently against the satin.

"That feels nice, doesn't it?" I said happily, and something came to me: stimulation . . . invigoration . . . awakening of the senses — pleasant sensations! Why, this is easy! Ideas began to surface quickly. I grabbed a pencil to write them down:

- A warm, tranquil bubble bath for Seth — by candlelight with iridescent bubbles rising to the ceiling.
- Rubbing a frozen block of sweet, tart orange juice against his lips and gums on a summer day.
- Giving him a handful of fresh, smooth rose petals to play with till they become wilted and damp.
- Dangling his little feet in a big bowl of dry kidney beans.

That list has continued to grow, while our son has grown into a happy, sparkling-eyed two-and-a-half-year-old with mischief on his mind. And his mommy — that's me — has learned that when God arrives with the comfort he promises, it may be something as simple as pleasant memories. With his help, we're working to make more of them every day.

When we accept tough jobs . . .
miracles can happen.
— ARLAND GILBERT

ONE POUND
NINE OUNCES
SANDY GARREDO

At last the nurse gave in to my desperate questions. "She weighs one pound nine ounces," she said.

The probing lights of the delivery room blurred over my head as unconsciousness stole over me. When I awakened, I was back in my room. My husband, Barry, stepped quickly to my bedside.

"Tell me the truth about the baby," I said. "Tell me everything."

A distant look came over Barry's face as he tried to separate his emotions from the medical facts he'd been bombarded with. "The doctor gives her a twenty percent chance of living. Even if she makes it, she'll probably have brain damage and have all kinds of other problems. The doctor says she's just too small."

Barry stared at the wall as he began to repeat himself. "The doctor says the chances are slim she'll live and even slimmer that she'll be normal if she does live." He turned to me uncertainly. "Sandy . . . do . . . don't you want to see her now?"

I closed my eyes and formed the word "no." *Better not,* said my anxious, tired brain. *Don't get attached. Just rest.*

But I slept fitfully. When the nurses caught me awake, they kept asking if I wanted to see her. It had been twenty-four hours now and I still hadn't seen Kara. She was Kara, not "it." And she was three months premature.

I thought back to what my obstetrician had told me when I'd begun dilating at only five months. "It all depends," he said carefully, "on how long we can keep from delivering that baby. Chances of survival are fair if we can make it to seven months and if the baby weighs at least two-and-a-half pounds."

Then, only a month later, the contractions began. In spite of surgery and medication — and prayers — the baby was

144

coming far, far too soon. I had pleaded with the Lord that this would not happen. I believed in prayer, and our church was very strong in prayer. But now I felt so frightened it was hard even to pray.

Barry came quietly into the room and sat down beside my bed, taking my hand. "I've been to see her," he said.

I was mute, questioning him with my eyes. "Tiny," he said softly, "so tiny. She's red as a rose and just thirteen inches long. She's in an isolette — it's like a small greenhouse for premature babies — and they've got a kind of little cellophane cap on her head to help retain body heat."

"Is she any . . . stronger?" I asked.

Barry looked away. "Well, she's down to one-pound-six," he answered, "but they say a weight loss is normal right after birth."

I gripped Barry's hand. He was working so hard at being brave. But I was more afraid than he was. Still, I was being selfish. I shouldn't allow my fear to weigh him down. "I — I'll go see her now," I said in a trembly voice.

The tires of my wheelchair turned rhythmically as Barry pushed it toward the ICU nursery — *one pound six ounces, one pound six ounces, one pound six ounces . . .*

We passed the viewing windows of the nursery. Each isolette had its own thicket of tubes and respirators, pumps and monitors for heartbeat and breathing. Alert to each set of beeps and flashing lights, the nurses worked one-on-one, guarding each little life.

A nurse showed us where to wash our hands and put on the sterile gowns she'd given us. Finally we were beside our baby's isolette. Despite Barry's having tried to prepare me, a current of shock jolted through me as I stared at the fragile little figure before me. Her head was smaller than my cupped hand.

When the baby's breathing monitor sounded, the attending nurse quickly reached in through a sleeve opening in the isolette to revive her. The woman was so calm! And then she asked the unthinkable. "Would you like to hold her?"

I was frozen. But Barry nodded, and the nurse got a blanket out of something that looked like a big bun-warmer and wrapped the baby up, tubes and all. Barry reached out and nestled her close. After a few moments he turned and extended the bundle to me.

I took it. The blanket seemed to wrap around something that wasn't there. Yet the instant I cradled her in my arms I felt a vibrancy, a magnetism that made me draw it close to my breast, my heart. Kara. Peeping between the folds, I saw her exquisitely sculpted face, a baby in miniature. I held her close within the circle of my arms, and the essence of my baby seemed to soak into my skin, making my very blood warmer.

Holding Kara, this baby God had created just for me, I felt a holy bond between us. The fear that tormented me before had gone.

I'd been afraid to love Kara for fear of losing her. But God had shown me that His love can't be limited by conditions or problems. Kara was His gift to me, and I knew in this instant that God would only give me something good. Whatever lay ahead, Kara was my child and God's child, and He would care for us both.

Lord, help me to remember that nothing is going to happen today that you and I cannot handle.
— Author Unknown

"Lord, Keep My Kids Safe"
Mae Bertha Carter

I woke up that September morning so filled with fear I could barely get out of bed. Matthew, my husband, was already up. He had fetched water from the pump, heated it up on the stove, and was filling the tub in the bedroom. Our five older children washed and got dressed while Matthew bathed our two youngest girls. I cooked breakfast. The kids were unusually quiet, no one talking excitedly about the first day of school. But then, school usually started for them in November, after most of the cotton had been picked.

Out of a wadded handkerchief I took

seven quarters for lunch money and gave one to each of them — Deborah, Beverly, Pearl, Gloria, Stanley, Larry and Ruth. Then we waited on the front porch for the school bus.

Normally they would have been out in the cotton fields working. We worked from "can to can't," sunrise to sunset. Other families stopped picking on Fridays at noon. Not us Carters. We worked right through the weekend until Saturday night: four bales a week. Even after school, if there was any cotton left, the children picked. But I had decided I didn't want them stuck in a sharecropper's life.

I finally spotted the school bus coming our way. Not a rusty old hand-me-down, but a brand-new, yellow school bus. It stopped in front of our house. My kids were the first on. How would the other children react when they saw them there?

The fear came over me again. I watched the bus disappear down the road, then I went inside and lay across our bed. *Lord,* I prayed, *take care of my kids. Take care of my kids. Take care of my kids.* There have been times when I have felt God's covering, when I've sensed a protective peace all around. That was not one of them. My children had gone off to school. The only black children to enter a white school in Drew, Mississippi.

In 1965, the local school board — under court order — instituted something called freedom of choice. That summer, when the cotton wasn't open yet, and the only work we had to do was tend our own vegetable garden, I was off visiting relatives in St. Louis the day the choice notices arrived at the farm. My girl Ruth opened the letter and made up her mind right away. She wanted to go to the white school. She talked to the other kids and one by one they came to the same decision. All Matthew and I could say was, "If you want to go, we want you to go."

Early on August 12, Matthew and I put on our best clothes, climbed into our pickup, and drove the nine miles into Drew. The town was quiet, but I felt as if everyone were peeking out of their windows at us. We stopped at the white high school, which was clean and freshly painted. It was the first time I had ever been inside. A secretary showed us into the principal's office. When we handed him the papers he got all red and flustered, but didn't say anything. We had no idea we were the only black parents in the county who had chosen to desegregate a school.

Word got out. The next day the plantation overseer, Mr. Thornton, drove up. "It's starting," Matthew muttered as he headed outside. I overheard Mr. Thornton telling my husband our kids could get a better education at the black school, and the white kids wouldn't talk to them, and black folks wouldn't have anything to do with us either.

I got so riled up I went inside and picked up a portable record player and a record my oldest son had given me of a President Kennedy speech about civil rights. I set the player on a chair near the door and turned the volume up so Mr. Thornton could hear Mr. Kennedy saying, "We are confronted primarily with a moral issue. It is as old as the Scriptures and is as clear as the American Constitution." We would not back down.

A few nights later Matthew was awakened at 3:00 a.m. by the sound of crunching gravel. He looked out the front window. "What on earth?" he muttered. The next thing I knew, I was jolted out of bed by the pop-pop-pop of gunfire. *Lord, have mercy.* Bullets flew across the porch, shattering the windows. Bullets hit the wall above the bed where two of the kids were asleep. Scrambling through the house,

Matthew and I brought all the kids to the back room. There we lay on the floor out of sight. The cars roared off, but we stayed put until dawn while Matthew sat by the front door, his shotgun in his lap.

I didn't know where to turn. I didn't feel I could trust any folk of authority in Drew. I had my husband drive me to Cleveland, the next town over, and I spoke to Mr. Moore, the head of the NAACP there. He notified the deputy sheriff of the county, and the FBI visited and took the bullets out of our walls as evidence. They promised there would be an investigation. But how would we sleep knowing someone wanted to do us harm?

The next night we returned to the back room, all of us huddled on the floor. I prayed and prayed for the Lord's covering. *Lord, keep my kids safe.* I also prayed, *Lord, help us eat.* That same day Matthew had gone to the country store, the only place we could buy on credit when we needed it. The manager took one look at my husband and said, "I'll give you until three o'clock to get your children out of the white school." When Matthew came home, I dug out the forty dollars I had saved under our mattress, so he could shop at another store. How much longer could we survive?

For four nights we slept in the back room, me worrying myself sick. Then one evening I recalled something I once heard a preacher say: "Everybody's afraid, and it's okay to be afraid, but you can't let fear stop you." No, I couldn't. And I wouldn't. People could complain and harass us all they wanted; we wouldn't be stopped. Like a blanket wrapped around each sleeping child, the covering of the Lord came over us. *Thank you, Lord,* I prayed. I slept better than I had in weeks, and the next night we returned to our bedrooms.

We worked hard preparing for the start of school. We picked cotton during the day, and in the evenings we readied the children's school clothes. No one would be able to say our children weren't neat and clean. Matthew had learned to sew from his mother; at night he made underwear for the girls out of flour sacks.

Help came from people we didn't even know. One day I was visiting friends down the road, and my daughter Beverly came running. "Mama," she said, "there's a white lady and a black lady waiting for you." Total strangers, they had heard about our situation. They said they were from New York and they were trying to help people like us. After taking plenty of notes and inspecting our bullet holes, they promised to tell our story and raise money from lodges, churches, synagogues, and other groups up north.

But on September 3, 1965, the first day of school, after sending my kids off on the bus, I felt alone and afraid. I lay on the bed for hours, praying *Lord, keep my children safe.* When they finally burst through the door that afternoon I was so glad to see them again. I sat them down and made them tell me everything about their day. It hadn't been easy, but no way would they give up.

That fall I prayed every moment I could. Sometimes the children told me about being called "nigger" or having spitwads thrown at them. Once the bus driver told them to sit at the back of the bus, but they stayed up front. It broke my heart when Ruth told me one day, "I hate them. I hate those white folks."

"Ruth," I told her, "don't say that. Hate destroys you. Don't hate."

I could tell that Ruth was hurt. All fall Matthew and I continued to work in the fields, counting every penny we earned. As usual, we hoped to collect a few extra bales for ourselves by following behind the automatic picking machines. But that October, someone attached a disc to the tractor, which plowed the last of the cotton under. On December 10, the overseer told us we were ninety-seven dollars in debt, and that there was no more land for us to work. We would have to move.

Even then I couldn't hate because the covering had come back. God was with us, and I knew in spite of everything we would be all right. We would find another place to live. We would find another way to earn a living. We had stepped out in faith, and God would not let us down.

We moved into Drew, where Matthew got a job. From then on all our children attended Drew High School. Seven of them eventually graduated from Ole Miss.

A lot has changed since 1965. The world's a different place. These days people tell me I showed a lot of courage back then. I have to tell them it came with the Lord's covering. That's something that never changes.

Poor and content is rich, and rich enough.
— WILLIAM SHAKESPEARE

PATENT LEATHER OXFORDS
ELINORE HAGLUND

While in the store recently, I watched a small child with a very bored expression on her little face choosing three pairs of shoes in varied colors. Her well-dressed, preoccupied mother sat next to her on the edge of the chair, alternately looking at her watch and urging the child to make up her mind. The child obliged, and the pair left the store hurriedly, the mother carrying three boxes and her daughter running behind, both appearing relieved that another tiresome task had been accomplished.

Watching them took me back to a memorable Saturday night when, as a child of six, I received my first pair of black patent leather oxfords. It also made me realize

156

that affluence can cause loss rather than gain, and that having more is not the guaranteed path to pleasure and fulfillment.

My widowed mother raised her five children in a small town in the Midwest. We were what was considered a poor family, although I cannot remember any unhappiness or discontent.

The main street of our town was a block long, with stores on either side. Saturday was the only night of the week that the stores were open. This was not just the end of the work week, it was a community event. The streets were brightly lit and filled with people of all ages. The women shopped for groceries and other goods for the home, met their friends, and chatted; the men stood in groups, discussing the weather or crops, and the children darted in and out among them. We spent the evening running up one side of the street and down the other, going in and out of stores and pressing our faces against the windows to admire the displays inside. It was on such a night that I first saw the patent leather oxfords; from then on, I noticed little else.

In our family we each had one pair of shoes at a time and we knew they would not be replaced until the soles and heels were completely beyond repair. At the time I saw the oxfords in the window, my high-topped ones were wearing thin, and I knew that because I was due to start school that year, they would have to be replaced. When I showed the oxfords to my older sister, her remark was, "Well, they're patent leather and you know that cracks, so they wouldn't last long enough."

For several successive Saturday nights I stood in front of the window of the general store admiring the shoes, oblivious to my friends running up and down the street behind me. After what my sister told me, I felt sure that the shoes were unattainable, and I never even mentioned them to my mother. But still, I stared and dreamed of my feet encased in their shining smoothness.

Then the night came when Mother said, "Tonight, we must go and get your new school shoes."

We went into the general store hand in hand, and I sat down to wait my turn. When I heard Mother tell the clerk, "We would like to see a pair of the black patent leather oxfords in the window," I shivered in anticipation. When they were put on my feet, I could hardly stand on my trembling legs, ankles cool and free of the restricting leather and laces of my old high-topped shoes.

Still, feeling I must warn her, I said to Mother, "But Winnie says they crack and won't last."

Mother smiled, squeezed my hand, and answered, "We'll just take them anyway."

I left the store, both arms wrapped around the shoe box, cradling it like a baby close to my heart. My night was complete. Every few steps I smiled up at Mother until she burst out laughing and asked, "Did you think I didn't know what you were looking at in that window every Saturday night?" She put her arm around my shoulders, pulling me so close that I felt her long skirt swish against my legs the rest of the way home.

Before going to sleep, I removed the shoes from the box and placed them on top of the old sewing machine just opposite my bed. I wanted them to be the first thing I saw when I opened my eyes Sunday morning. It took quite a while to arrange them, as I couldn't decide whether to have the shiny toes facing me, or to have them sideways so that I could see all of them at one glance. Finally they were placed to my satisfaction and I snuggled under my patchwork quilt and looked at them until all the lights were out.

I do not recall now if they "lasted," but I am sure that no precious jewel has ever shone more brightly or made anyone happier than did those shoes shining softly in the sun when I opened my eyes the next morning.

One of the best ways to demonstrate
God's love is to listen. . . .
— Bruce Larsen

MAMA'S ROOM
Carol Bessent Hayman

Mama's room was always the big front bed-room just to the left as you entered the two-story frame house with its sprawling porches on three sides, upstairs and down. Somehow we always gravitated there, and it became more living room to us than the parlor across the hall or the dining room with its wrought-iron daybed behind the parlor.

Each morning, Mama fluffed her big featherbed — the focal point of the room — into a cloudy mass and topped it with two snowy white feather pillows. Mama was very particular about her bed. You did not sit or loll about on it; and it was a treat of treats to get to sleep in this confection, which always felt just as good as it looked.

An assortment of furniture clustered

161

around the bed, and several rocking chairs waited nearby, one of which we referred to as "Mama's chair." When the day's work ended and she could rest, we always knew we could find her here. It was here that I came with my confidences and my problems, and it was here that I brought my little joys and sorrows, for nothing seemed complete until it had been shared with Mama. She always listened as if each word I said had importance, and her opinion was always wise and full of love for me.

It is but right that our hearts
should be on God, when the heart
of God is so much on us.
— RICHARD BAXTER

A NEW MOTHER'S REFLECTIONS ON GOD'S LOVE

KATHRYN SLATTERY

Katy lies napping, cradled in my left arm. Sleeping babies look like plump, furled flower buds, I've often thought. But on this July afternoon, with every heat and humidity record being broken, I feel no rosy raptures of motherhood. Hot, tired, crabby, and frustrated are more like it. For the six weeks of Katy's life, my life has been a monotonous round of changing diapers, waking three times a night for feedings, soothing her cries.

Now she has finally drifted off in the crook of my arm after twenty minutes of

163

fussing. I sit at the dining room table, my free right hand busily scribbling the first of scores of long overdue thank-you notes. An unfamiliar noise causes me to look up. *Cruncha-cruncha-cruncha.* Across the room our cat, Indy, is nibbling at the leaves of our one healthy potted plant.

I want to yell a loud, outraged *Shoo!* I ache to jump up and chase that mischief till she scuttles to a hiding place under the bed. But wake Katy? Impulsively my fingers close around the blue-striped pen in my hand and I fling it toward the cat. It hits the wall above the plant and clatters to the floor. Indy regards me coolly and continues to nibble green leaves.

I sit still and squeeze my eyes shut, ashamed. Warm drops run into the corners of my mouth. I take a shaky breath.

I'm sorry, God. Not very grown-up of me, was it? Sometimes being a mother makes me feel so overwhelmed. Helpless.

I lean back in the chair and look down at Katy. This fragile bud of a human being. My daughter. I remember so clearly the feeling that came over me the night Tom and I brought her home from the hospital. We leaned on the rails of her crib, watching her sleep in her new home for the first time. I looked at that sweet face, the perfectly modeled fingers and toes, and felt millions of tiny dancing bubbles well up inside of me: a different kind of love. Not like my love for Tom. Or for my father or mother or sister. This love was newborn, like my baby. It filled me with a fierce tenderness. I would do anything to protect this tiny creature, so dependent on me for her life.

The memory is good. Like a gentle hand taking mine. And as I look down on Katy now, something dawns on me.

Without you, God, I'm as helpless as Katy. You take care of me, giving me strength to take care of Katy.

It's late in the summer now and the heat is disappearing. I'm in the basement doing laundry. Katy is upstairs asleep in her crib. Suddenly I hear her cry. There is an anguished note in it, as if she feels utterly abandoned. Slamming the dryer door shut, I dash up the stairs and into the nursery and take her in my arms.

"There, there," I croon, holding her close to my breast, the soft curve of her head in the hollow under my chin. "Please don't cry. Mommy's always here — always. I'll never leave you, my Katy."

Standing in her sunlit room, kissing away her tears, I hear a vaguely familiar ring in my words of reassurance to Katy. We settle into the rocking chair, and as we relax in its soothing rhythm, back and forth, back and forth, it comes to me — Jesus' promise to his disciples after the Resurrection. "I am with you always" (Matthew 28:20, NRSV).

Dear God, you always hear me when I cry out. You are always there, aren't you?

Almost a year has passed. Katy is beginning to walk. Sitting cross-legged on the lawn, I watch my intrepid explorer start up the steps leading to the wooden deck at the back of the house. At the base of the steps is a slab of poured concrete. Poised on the first step, Katy turns to face me, her eyes shining with pride in her accomplishment. Her legs, unsteady, begin to wobble. . . .

Even before I move to catch her, I know it is too late. Down she goes, face first, whacking her forehead on the concrete.

"Katy!"

Her brow is scraped and bleeding, already purple with an ugly bruise. She is screaming, and as I pick her up, nightmarish fears crowd my mind: concussion . . . skull fracture . . . brain damage . . .

Still holding Katy, I race up the steps and into our bedroom, where the well-worn copy of *Dr. Spock's Baby and Child Care* lies waiting in the bookcase. Katy's cries seem to be subsiding as I scan the book's pages about head injuries. According to Dr. Spock, Katy is showing no symptoms of having suffered anything serious. I sponge her forehead with a cool washcloth and hold her on my lap murmuring words of love. Minutes later she is all smiles, playing with Indy as though nothing had happened.

But I am still shaken.

Oh, God, I feel Katy's pain so deeply. Suddenly I grasp something of the magnitude of your love for us. Your children. I cry when I think that you loved us so much that you let your Son live . . . and suffer . . . and die . . . for us.

A crisp fall morning, a morning when little nuisances have stolen the time. Within the hour Tom will be home from the office, and we are supposed to be off for our long-awaited weekend in the country. But Katy is still in her nightgown. Seated in her highchair, she has more egg in her hair and on her face than in her tummy, and she is blissfully oblivious to our need to hurry.

Across the room the television is on. A big letter "K" dances across the screen and

Katy catches sign of it. She throws her hands skyward — launching a full mug of milk across the dining room.

"Katy —"

I am about to scold, but I catch myself. In recent days I've noticed how sensitive Katy seems to my reprimands, especially when my tone is harsh.

Katy regards me warily.

"Katy," I repeat quietly, bending over to pick up the empty mug. "Do you know what you say when you spill your milk?" Smiling, I touch her tousled head. "You say, 'Oops!' "

A big sunny grin lights Katy's face; I wipe up the floor, feeling so thankful for not giving in to irritation.

Father God, your love is never corrupted by moods or time pressure or any of our human foibles. You love me in my worst moments and, in your perfect love, offer me forgiveness.

I look at the little figure in the highchair. Katy has created a new love in me, mother love. She has given me fresh glimpses of our Creator's love for all his children. A love that is protective, ever present, sacrificing, forgiving.

Thank you, Almighty Father.

We are here to add what we can to life,
not to get what we can from it.
— SIR WILLIAM OSLER

MY CINDERELLA GRANDMOTHER
KATHLEEN M. GILBERT

If opportunity and circumstance had not been obstacles in my grandmother's life, she would have become a famous fashion designer. She would have purchased exquisite fabrics to dress the world's most beautiful women, choreographed extravagant fashion shows, attended lavish banquets, and lived a Cinderella life of gold, glass, and glitter. Instead, Grandmother was to spend her life venting her creativity on her daughter and granddaughter.

Grandmother became familiar with the clothing industry while she was employed as a seamstress in New York City's garment district. It was there that she would tediously cut and sew pieces of material together all day long for most of her life. With no opportunity for self-expression, she performed the repetitive tasks like an assembly-line robot of the early twentieth century. It was in these minutes and hours that she would mentally design our stylish clothing.

Mother and I spent countless hours with Grandmother as she tailored her patterns to our unique figures. Grandmother was so fluid in her movements as she pinned us from collar to hem. She was like a whirlwind, moving from her knees to a standing position while tucking fabric under her chin or arms and pulling out lengths to be measured. And as she stuffed her lips with the heads of pins, she would mumble, "Kathleen, never put pins in your mouth. You could swallow them!"

Our times together became a tradition as we shared plenty of good food, good conversation, and good laughs. There was usually a pot of Grandmother's tomato sauce filled with meatballs and sausage simmering on the stove and other delicacies like baked, garlic-stuffed mushrooms and artichokes just waiting to be eaten. We'd laugh at ourselves over the silliest things — especially as we grew more tired, for Grandmother worked relentlessly for hours on end. Getting stuck with pins wasn't one of my favorite things, but it was inevitable and guaranteed a round of laughter.

Grandmother would never lose her concentration as she went from us to the sewing machine, then to the ironing board and back to us again, all the while in conversation. She had to finish what she began. Even though Mother's and my stamina would begin to wane in the late hours of the evening, there would usually be one last touch that needed to be added. And when the garment was completed to Grandmother's satisfaction, she would stand back and have us turn around and around. Then she would compliment us on how beautiful we looked in our new clothing! There were times, however, when her passion for the art kept her up and sewing long after we'd gone home. Her creativity was free to soar within the confines of her home during those peaceful early hours of the morning.

Grandmother must have found much more contentment in dressing us than she ever could have dressing temperamental models. Perhaps her life was like Cinderella's after all, in that she found enjoyment and fulfillment in being with and doing for her loved ones.

Letting Go

Don't laugh at a youth for his affectations. He is only trying on one face after another to find his own.
— LOGAN PEARSALL SMITH

LETTING GO
SUE MONK KIDD

When my daughter Ann entered her teens, we went through a brief but stormy adjustment period. One morning she came out of her room wearing an odd combination of clothes. "You're not going to school like *that*, are you?" I asked.

She planted her feet. "I was planning on it!" I insisted she change. She resisted. Our voices rose. Before she left we were both practically in tears.

Later when my friend Betty called, I mentioned the episode. "Be honest," she said. "Was it really her choice of clothes that was bothering you?"

Sure it was, I thought. But all day the question needled me. Finally I sat in Ann's room and tried to figure it out. As I stared at her closet, I remembered how I used to dress her myself. That's when my honest moment came. I knew my daughter was trying to discover her independence. What was *really* bothering me was that she was growing up.

That evening I revealed my honest moment to Ann. "Be patient with me," I said. "It's hard letting go."

"I know, Mama," she said. "It's hard for me, too. Sometimes I wish I was still small enough for you to dress." Then she wound her arms around me and squeezed tight.

*Draw nigh to God
and he will draw nigh to you . . .*
— JAMES 4:8

I KNOW YOU'LL BE OKAY
CAROL KUYKENDALL

"Mom, please don't go." Twelve-year-old Kendall gripped my arm as we stood by the car in the camp parking lot that summer Sunday afternoon. "I'm scared."

Any mother who's heard those words from her child knows the instinctive response. I wanted to wrap my arms around her, to comfort and protect her from her fears. But almost as instinctively, I knew I should not.

"I *know* you'll be okay," I said, trying to sound confident in spite of my own shaky emotions.

"How do you *know?*"

"I just do," I replied. "Jesus will be with you."

At that moment, a counselor and some

kids walked by. "C'mon, Kendall!" they called. She seemed immobile, so I made the first move. "Good-bye, sweetie," I said, hugging her and then quickly getting into the car and driving away without looking back. I ached for Kendall, but I kept remembering the words of a wise friend: "Sometimes our children learn to depend upon the Lord only when we get out of the way."

Throughout the week, I didn't know who was suffering most, but when I picked up Kendall on Saturday, I got my answer. "Mom, this was the *best* week of my life!"

*Mothering invites the habit
of prayer for prayer . . .*
— MURSHIDA VERA, JUSTIN CORDA

FIRST DAY OF SCHOOL
NANCY A. CARLSON

Dear Lord,

My little girl starts school tomorrow. She is anxious and excited. I doubt that she'll sleep a wink tonight. Help her, please, to quiet down and try to rest.

Lord, bless her tomorrow as she puts on her new dress and shoes. We've walked the route to school many times this summer, so I know she knows the way. She's an independent youngster, Lord, but please let her allow me to walk with her just this once.

Be with her, Lord, as she goes inside the school. Let her not be lonely or afraid in this new and challenging world. Be with her teacher; help my little one to be respectful and appreciative. And, oh Lord, be with me, for a whole new aspect of my education is also beginning. Tomorrow I start learning how to let my daughter go. There is no better way than to entrust her into your care.

Well, Lord, it's quiet in her room now. I think she's fallen asleep . . . thank you. Amen.

*Now this is the day. Our child, into the
daylight you will go out standing.*
— ZUNI PRAYER

I'LL DRIVE, MOM!
CAROL KUYKENDALL

"Hi, Mom — I'll drive!" Lindsay greeted me
cheerfully that bright spring afternoon as she
opened the car door and tossed her school-
books on the backseat.

"Hmmm?" I answered, playing dumb
and gazing at my almost-sixteen-year-old
daughter. She had just received her
learner's permit, a piece of paper that gave
her permission to change places with me in
the car so I could teach her how to drive —
on real streets, in real traffic. Exciting for
Lindsay. Heart-stopping for me.

"You sure you want to?" I asked doubt-
fully, looking around the high school
parking lot, which had suddenly come alive
with the sounds of exuberant teenagers
and screeching tires. I might as well have

asked if she was sure she wanted to grow up, or go to the senior prom.

"Oh, Moth-*er!*" she replied in the exasperated voice she used when I asked the absurdly obvious.

I shrugged hesitantly and slid all the way over to the passenger seat. *Why does that seem like such a long slide?* I asked myself as I watched my girl-child climb in and scoot the seat forward until the steering wheel nearly touched her shoulders. She honked the horn and waved to a friend, turned the key in the ignition, and pulled the shift lever into reverse. Suddenly we shot backward and jolted to a stop.

That's when I knew why it was a long slide. I was afraid. Afraid of how car keys suddenly change a child into an adult. Afraid of the responsibility of trying to teach her all she needed to know. And afraid that when it was time for her to drive off by herself, she wouldn't be ready.

"Whoa, sorry about the whiplash there," Lindsay said with a grin.

"Just be careful — and don't forget your seat belt," I said, clicking my own into place. I felt like a test pilot gearing up for a trial run with a rookie. I concentrated on my deep breathing, the kind I practiced for relaxation during labor pains before Lindsay was born.

"Mom, you worry too much," Lindsay told me as she shifted into drive.

She was right, of course. Worrying had always been an important part of my job description as a parent. If she said "head-ache," I thought CAT scan. If she said "stomach ache," I feared appendectomy. If I heard a siren and she wasn't home, I wondered if I could get to the emergency room before she did. I prayed and told God I was giving him my fears, but I didn't.

Lindsay eased out of the parking lot and onto the highway, gathering speed as we went down a small hill.

"Slow down!" I cautioned, sneaking a look at the speedometer.

"Mom, I'm going the speed limit," Lindsay informed me with exaggerated patience.

In the distance I could see a four-way stop. "Be careful!" I warned again, putting my hands on the dashboard to brace for the sudden stop. Instead, we slowed down gently. "The car on your right has the right-of-way," I instructed, "but defensive driving means expecting the unexpected. Always look both ways!"

Lindsay nodded and moved forward smoothly. "See, Mom, I can do it!" she said with a confident smile.

When we finally pulled into our driveway, I felt like the mother in the cartoon taped to our refrigerator door. The smiling teenager is climbing out from behind the wheel of the car. "Thanks for the lesson, Mom!" the caption reads. Meanwhile, the mother is seated on the passenger side with a look of terror frozen on her face and her feet thrust right through the floorboards. I laughed when I cut it out. That was before Lindsay got her permit.

The next few outings, I didn't feel much better. In merging traffic, I closed my eyes and prayed. On narrow country roads, I was sure Lindsay was about to shear off the mailboxes on my side of the road. In free-for-all shopping center parking lots, I reminded her to look both ways.

As Lindsay's birthday approached, I tried to think of an appropriate gift to mark this milestone celebration and decided upon a key chain with her own set of keys to our car. I searched the stores, but all I could find were ones that said, "Let's party!" or "I love weekends."

"We could engrave your own message on

one of these," a salesman suggested, showing me several plain ones.

"Perfect!" I decided, choosing a gold heart.

"What do you want to say on it?" he asked.

I paused, thinking of Lindsay alone in the car without my advice.

"Look both ways," I told him.

The morning of Lindsay's birthday, we celebrated with candles in doughnuts and presents at breakfast. "Look both ways!" she repeated when she opened the box containing her own set of car keys. "How could I ever forget, Mom? It seems like you've been telling me that all my life."

Later that day, after she passed her driving test and got her official license, obviously her best present of all, she drove me home and then asked if she could take the car over to a friend's house.

This was the moment I'd feared. Her maiden voyage. Alone.

"It's okay, Mom!" she assured me. "I can do it."

I merely nodded, fearful of the sound of my voice.

As I watched her pull out of the driveway, I thought of Jochebed, Moses's mother, who placed her little baby in a basket and let him float down the Nile River. She knew the dangers that lurked in those waters. But once out of her grasp and out of her control, she had to stand back and watch him go, trusting he was in God's hands.

I'd done all I could do. Probably I made some mistakes. Probably I left some things out. But now it was time to let go and trust. Besides, I thought with a faint smile, she had her keychain message, "Look both ways."

That's good advice for me too, I thought. Look down at the fear, and then look up to God. Knowing that I'd done the best I could, it was time to trust him.

Praying always with all prayer and
supplication in the Spirit . . .
— EPHESIANS 6:18

STAYING CLOSE THROUGH PRAYER
PAMELA KENNEDY

I was talking with another mother recently, and we were discussing our children. She has two grown sons who live far from home. "Isn't it difficult," I asked, "to maintain that closeness you had when they were home?" She admitted it was at times, but shared her secret of how to feel near to them.

"Every day I talk to God about them. Sometimes I ask Him to give them good friends or wisdom in making decisions or discernment at work. Just because they are far away doesn't mean I can't be an influence in their lives."

She had captured the essence of prayer as Paul expressed it in his letter to the believers at Ephesus. At all times, prayer keeps the hopes, praises, and concerns we have for those we love in the forefront of our minds and hearts.

We cannot always be with our children. Then we can pray for God to direct them. Our advice may not always be welcomed. Then we can pray for the Holy Spirit to guide them. Our children may not be aware of how much they owe their heavenly Father. Then we can offer our prayers of praise on their behalf. Prayer is a powerful opportunity for each of us. As mothers we have the privilege and obligation to pray. We can remain close to our children in heart and mind as we pray for them at *all times* with *all kinds* of prayers.

*I have learned, in whatsoever state I am,
therewith to be content.*
— PHILIPPIANS 4:11

CONTENTMENT
MARION BOND WEST

For years grocery shopping was a grueling task. I'd hurry through the store putting anything in sight into my cart. I didn't dare indulge in the luxury of reading labels for fear one of my twin sons would jump out of the cart. One day one of the twins escaped and the manager had to make an announcement over the loudspeaker. That same day the other twin threw a jar of dill pickles out of the cart and broke it.

I never got accustomed to the stares of women with one well-behaved child. I admired others who shopped without children. They had grocery lists, organized coupons, manicured nails, and carefully applied makeup. They strolled leisurely through the grocery store smiling at everyone. So unlike me!

Now — my children all grown — I grocery shop alone. I can take all the time I want and read labels too. Funny thing. I find myself watching women struggle through the store with whining, rambunctious children and I envy them. I want to go back to the way it used to be. I told my daughter Julie and she happily loaned me her two little ones to take grocery shopping, but she gave me a bit of advice too:

"Mother, you have to be content with who you are in life. Don't look back and yearn for the past. I love and admire you just the way you are now!"

*One can know nothing of giving aught
that is worthy to give unless one also
knows how to take.*
— Havelock Ellis

Learning to Accept
Marilyn Morgan Helleberg

My daughter Karen lives alone and works full time, so I often invite her to eat lunch with me. Recently, though, she asked me to dinner at her house, and I discovered a surprising thing: I had a rather hard time letting her be the giver! On the way to her house, I thought, "Karen's just making ends meet. I shouldn't eat food that she's bought with her hard-earned money."

Then a memory flashed before my mind. It was my first year of teaching and my bank account was running on empty. Mother had come to town to shop, and I'd offered to take her out for lunch. I can still see the blue and white tablecloth under our hands as we both reached for the check. Our eyes met. Mother swallowed hard, smiled, and said, "Thank you." I don't think I have ever felt so straight and tall as I did that day as I walked to the cash register.

When I got to Karen's house, she made me sit down and let her serve me, even though I offered to help. I allowed it because I want her to know how it feels to walk straight and tall.

Do you insist on always being the giver in your relationships? Maybe today you'll have a chance to give the harder gift: letting the other person give to you!

Love,
   Your Daughter

*At any moment in life we have the option
to choose an attitude of gratitude,
a posture of grace, a commitment to joy.*
— TIM HANSEL

FIELDS OF
YELLOW DAISIES
CAROL KUYKENDALL

The summer day dawned bright and clear. A perfect morning to start a family vacation. And everyone was filled with excited anticipation. Everyone, that is, except me.

As we pulled out of the driveway and onto the highway, headed for Montana, I felt the same dull weight of depression I'd carried around for weeks, ever since my mother died.

"Mommy," six-year-old Kendall asked, her face close to mine in the front seat, "are you going to be sad forever?"

"No, dear, of course not," I answered, forcing a smile. And again I vowed not to let my grief ruin the day. Or worse, ruin this vacation for my husband and our three children.

Please, Lord, I silently prayed, *help heal my sorrow. Help me to remember the joys of my mother's life and forget the pain she endured.* I had prayed variations of that prayer for the past six weeks, since the morning I held my mother's hand, easing her from life into death.

Mentally, I knew her death was a blessing. For years, she had suffered from emphysema. Since my father's death eight years before, she had lived next door to us, and though she and I had always been close, during those last years we became even closer. In her last months, as she grew weaker, I spent most of my time caring for her. She was tired, in pain, and ready to die. But in my heart, I was not ready to let her go. I suffered watching her suffer.

Briefly, just before the funeral, as family and friends gathered, I felt some solace. We all reminded one another of her happier, healthier days — riding horses on mountain trails, her love of laughter, her fierce family loyalty and unconditional love for all of us, even the silly little sayings she used to shape our lives as we were growing up.

"Think of fields of yellow daisies," was one of her favorites, and to me the most irritating. All throughout our childhood, she singsonged that little ditty to us whenever she expected us to rise bravely above our troubles.

Once she was driving us to the doctor's office for one of our regular polio vaccinations. My skin was crawling with the dread of the inevitable sting of the needle in my arm.

"Think of fields of yellow daisies," she cheerfully suggested, when I started complaining. That made me angry. The thought of yellow daisies didn't change how I felt. And besides, I had never even *seen* a field of yellow daisies.

I often thought my mother found God most vividly in nature. She even had all of us children baptized in a mountain meadow one bright summer day when we all were old enough to understand the significance of the ceremony.

After her funeral, family and friends went their separate ways, and the pace of my life slowed. That's when my depression descended, and now I couldn't seem to shake it. I felt like a sad child, orphaned by the loss of her mommy, and in many ways still dependent upon her emotionally.

Lord, I silently repeated, as our car sped along the highway, *I know I have to let go of the memory of her suffering, but I need help. Please give me some assurance that she is with you and free from pain now.*

It was a tall order for a prayer, I know. *Anyhow, with the Lord,* I said to myself, *all things are possible.* For the next two days we traveled through Colorado, Wyoming, and Montana. Finally we reached our destination, a cabin on the edge of a crystal-clear lake, rimmed by soft, purplish mountains.

"Surely this setting will lift your spirits," my husband, Lynn, said hopefully as we sat by the lake shortly after dawn the first morning.

"Surely it should," I agreed, trying to sound more cheerful than I felt.

"Let's hike up to that waterfall," he suggested, pointing to a cascade of water coming off a cliff at the far end of the lake.

I didn't feel like a hike at all.

"Come on, Mom!" the kids urged.

I knew I had no choice, so we started off around the lake and up the mountainside. As we climbed higher, the sound of water crashing over the rocks grew louder. The others ran on ahead, and I was the last one on the trail.

Slowly I rounded the last bend and came

in full view of the thundering falls. But it wasn't the sight of the cascading water that took my breath away. Tucked away to one side of the glistening falls, in the mist of the tumbling water, was a field of bright yellow daisies, the first I had ever seen in my whole life. I was overwhelmed, knowing at once that I had been blessed — not with a coincidence — but with a gift from God.

For a long time, I sat on a rock, drinking in the beauty beneath me. And, just as I am sure God intended, the grief began to ebb away.

And to this day, whenever I think of Mother, it is not pain and suffering and sorrow that I remember; it is the happy memories she gave me, like that precious field of yellow daisies.

Weep if you must, parting is here —
but life goes on, so sing as well.
— Joyce Grenfell

Mother's Lesson
Dale Evans Rogers

When my mother sat me down to help me get perspective on Debbie's death, she did not give me an involved spiritual argument. Instead, she painted a picture of a little girl bringing home flowers, a most familiar scene, and of God picking a flower for His garden. . . .

I could see and understand the implication of that picture. It made sense to me and restored my faith in a loving God.

*Nothing is really work unless you would
rather be doing something else.*
— Sir James M. Barrie

You Can Like
What You Do
Barbara Bush

My mother was a striking beauty who left the world a more beautiful place than she found it. She grew lovely flowers, did the finest needlepoint I have ever seen, and knew how to keep an exquisite home. . . .

She taught me a great deal, although neither of us realized it at the time. Probably her most important lesson was an inadvertent one. You have two choices in life: You can like what you do, or you can dislike it. I have chosen to like it.

*When God pardons, he consigns the
offense to everlasting forgetfulness.*
— MERV ROSELL

THE NOT FORGOTTEN
JEAN BELL MOSLEY

I try to remember the details of that long-ago day. They went something like this: Summer was over the land. I was barefoot, maybe seven or eight. The pink zinnias were in bloom. Mama was baking a special cake, my favorite, with little colored pillows of candy embedded in the icing. But as I look back, the cake was not important, nor the zinnias, nor my freed feet.

Desiring some teenage privacy from the rest of the family, my older sister had made a room for herself in a corner of the big log smokehouse. In a swept-out corner she had put a chair, a desk, a clumsy wooden-box bookcase. I could not understand this. In there along with the old smoky hams and strings of onions and hanks of dried pennyroyal! Why?

If my sister thought she had privacy, I could have told her she didn't, for some plaster had fallen from the chinks between the logs, and if I wanted to, I could see her every move. And from time to time I wanted to.

One day I didn't draw back quickly enough. My sister's shocked eyes bore into mine, at close range. Due report of my behavior was made, and Mama instructed me never to peek again.

But I did. There was another place the plaster was missing, a place where my sister wouldn't be expecting me to peek. All I could ever see that she was doing was reading a book.

This time I was caught, unexpectedly, from the rear, and Mama hauled me off to a place under the big cherry tree. Memory fades here. Was I spanked? Was I scolded? Shamed? Probably.

I do remember that when Mama was through with the "correction," she hugged me and said, "Now let's forget this ever happened." And I also remember the awful sinking feeling I had. I thought Mama would never again love me. I wandered off to the creek, waded awhile. But it wasn't fun. I went to the strawstack, crawled way back into a little cave the cows had made as they ate into it. It was suffocatingly hot, but I stayed for a long time, trying to do some sort of penance, I suppose. I thought about going to an abandoned log cabin about a mile away and staying there the rest of my life. I wished the lump in my throat would go away. I wished it were yesterday or tomorrow. I wished I hadn't disobeyed.

Soon I began to think of that cake Mama had baked. It was high and fluffy, and those little nuggets of sweetness on top! *My* cake. I wondered if dinnertime had come and gone. I could imagine the family gathered around the table, Dad saying, "I'll have another piece of the cake, please," and no one missing me. Not even Mama.

I went back to the house, looked quickly through the screen door. There was the cake, untouched, in the center of the table. I went around to look in a kitchen window, and then another one. Once, I felt sure Mama saw me, but she didn't say anything. I went again to the screen door and stood, this time long enough to be seen.

"Want to lick the icing bowl?" Mama asked, just like she always did.

I stepped inside and stood there by the door, wondering if I shouldn't say something. "Mama . . ." I began.

"Here, there's a lot left," she said, handing me the bowl and a spoon. She brushed the hair back out of my eyes. I looked into hers. There was no trace of disappointment, anger, or disapproval.

"But, Mama," I began again, feeling hot and sticky and throbbing with the necessity to say something more, to get the mighty hurt out of my throat.

"Hurry up," she said. "It'll soon be dinnertime. I want you to set the table."

"Mama, I won't do it again."

"Do what?"

"You know."

"Whatever you're talking about, I've forgotten." She busied herself with the potatoes.

I licked the bowl clean, wondering all the while if it really were possible to forget something like that, not over an hour old. I watched Mama furtively as she sliced the bread, poured the milk. Surely there would be some little telltale sign to show that she remembered my disobedience — a frown, a reference to my wrongdoing. She only smiled and hummed a little tune, just like always.

Yes, I supposed it was possible. My Mama could do anything. Never had I felt so wonderful, so free and airy, so everything-is-all-right.

"Can we use the rose-sprigged dishes?" I asked. They were our Sunday and special-occasion dishes.

Mama looked only a little puzzled. Then, looking around, she said, "Why, I suppose so. It's such a pretty day. You'll be careful."

The world, which had stopped for me, now moved on, better than ever. Old Tabby came out from behind the cook-stove, humped her back, and curled up in a spot of sunshine before the opened door. I picked a bouquet of pink zinnias for the table.

Over the years, Mama may have indeed forgotten that incident, but I haven't and hope I don't. It was my first glorious experience of what total forgiveness is like. Had she not demonstrated it, it may have been harder for me in later life to believe it could be done, harder for me to re-experience the ineffable peace, the joyous uplift that comes from knowing that confessed transgressions are forgotten by One who *really can* do anything, who can take these wrongdoings and hurl them into oblivion, which is somewhere as far as the east is from the west, the heavens from the earth. Rejoice!

*For anything worth having one must pay
the price; and the price is always work,
patience, love, self-sacrifice. . . .*
— JOHN BURROUGHS

MAMA HAD ALWAYS BEEN THERE
LINDA BROWN

I slid impatiently into the small car next to
my fiancé, Greg. Mama was standing on the
sidewalk outside the Brooklyn apartment
where she'd raised me, smiling hopefully.

"Good-bye, Mama," I said offhandedly.

When she leaned toward my rolled-down
car window to kiss me good-bye, I moved
my cheek slightly away. I didn't want her to
kiss me.

I'd hoped Greg couldn't see how hurt
Mama looked, but his light-blue eyes were
glancing curiously at me as we drove away.
I sat beside him silently, my back rigid
against the vinyl seat, my own dark eyes

fixed stubbornly on the shadows that flickered across the windshield.

"Linda," Greg said, "I know it was all
my idea to meet your mother . . ." I stared
stonily ahead.

"And I'm glad I did. She seems very
nice."

I still gave no response.

He sighed. "Well, frankly, I've never seen
you act this way. You were so cold. I don't
know what's gone on between you and
your mother, but I do know that there
must be a reason for the tension I saw."

A reason! How dare he judge me? I had
years of reasons, lists of reasons! But when
I turned to glare at him, I saw that his face
held no judgment, only quiet concern. His
hand left the steering wheel and tentatively
covered mine. And slowly, I began to tell
him about Mama — and Daddy . . .

In the 1950s, when I was growing up, my
father was a very troubled man. While
other children's fathers came back from
work in a stream of gray-flannel suits, my
father sat on the stoop in front of our
apartment building, wearing torn blue
jeans and a white T-shirt. He never held a
job. He'd just be sitting there, staring into
space, his hands cupping a lighted ciga-
rette.

Sometimes I would see the little girl who lived next door running to greet her father as he walked up the block with his shiny leather briefcase, and I would run into our apartment to hide my embarrassment. All my childish prayers revolved around my father: "Please, God, just let Daddy get better."

Mama's frustration grew with each unpaid bill she added to the pile on the kitchen shelf. Sunday mornings were the worst. While Daddy slept through the morning, Mama would throw a coat over her nightgown and run out to buy *The New York Times*. Then her red pen would come out. She'd sit at the white Formica table, with its pattern of tiny boomerangs, furiously circling ad after ad under "Help Wanted — Men." When she had covered the newsprint with bright-red circles, she'd take them to Daddy.

"Here are some jobs you could do!"

Daddy would only burrow more deeply under the old brown blanket. "I can't," he'd whisper. "Not this week."

One time Mama grabbed him by the shoulders. "We have no milk, no bread!" she pleaded.

Daddy stared at her helplessly. "Do you think I want to be like this?"

I believed he didn't. But Mama was too desperate to be sympathetic. Her lips pressed together in a thin line. The next Sunday, when she opened the *Times*, it was to "Help Wanted — Women."

But in the 1950s it was considered a gamble to hire a woman with small children. One night from the hushed darkness of the tiny room I shared with my sister, I heard her praying. When Mama had a problem, she wouldn't use fancy words; she's just say it straight out to God, like she was talking to a friend who hadn't ever let her down. "I'm a hard-working woman, God," she was saying. "Please don't let us go on welfare. I'll take any job I can get, even if it's for a tiny paycheck. I'll be the best worker they ever hired."

Eventually a friend of a friend gave Mama a secretarial job — and a warning: "I'm taking a chance on you. But if you plan on taking time off for every runny nose and blister your kids get, you can plan on finding another job."

Mama never took one day off. Even when my sister and I were miserably ill with the measles, she made it in to work. When we needed special care, we were trundled off to a neighbor's. I would lie feverishly on a couch there and hear her whisper loudly into her pink telephone, "What kind of mother goes off and leaves her children?" I didn't like this neighbor, but her attitude made me wonder about my mother.

Daddy grew worse and worse. Without Mama there to care for him, he became increasingly disoriented. I'd come home to find the apartment filled with smoke from cooking pots he'd left forgotten on the stove. I'd run around flinging windows open, terrified of what Mama might do if she found out.

One day I came home and found Mama there alone.

"Where's Daddy?"

"You could have been killed," she said reproachfully. "He could have set the house on fire."

"Where's Daddy?" I demanded.

"I sent him to the city hospital."

I raced to the door, as if he would still be there, but of course he wasn't.

"He was very sick, Linda. I had no choice. I can't look after all of you." She was, I supposed, trying to comfort me, but I ran away from her, inconsolable. The next day she was back at work, and Daddy had been placed in the psychiatric unit.

When my father was released from the

hospital, he didn't bother even trying to come home. His emotional problems and chronic depression made it impossible for him to face the pressures of family life. He lived alone, supporting himself with odd jobs. I blamed Mama for locking him out of our lives.

"You've got to forget the past," Mama would say when she noticed me looking particularly unhappy. But I couldn't forget. And I couldn't forgive her for sending my father away. Not a day went by when I didn't think, *If only she'd tried harder to help him. . . .*

Greg had almost reached my apartment now, and my voice was hoarse. "Has your mother forgiven your father?" he asked.

"No!" I launched into a diatribe on how Mama still spoke against Daddy. "She can't forget the past. She still blames him for things he couldn't help. She can't forgive, she won't forgive —"

"Well," Greg interrupted gently, "can you?"

"Of course I can! I have forgiven. I know my father couldn't help the way he was. He never meant to hurt us. He —"

"I meant," Greg said patiently, "can you forgive your mother?"

For many seconds the only sound was

the noise of the traffic outside the car windows. Me? Forgive my mother?

"You know, Linda," Greg said, breaking into my thoughts, "I've learned that times come in life when you have to make a really tough decision, a choice that is actually brutal. That's what happened to your mother. The situation got down to no food on the table, and was she going to take care of her husband or her kids? So she made that brutal choice. She had to choose between your father and you and your sister. She chose her children. She chose *you*."

I turned to look at Greg. What was he saying? *Mama chose me.* I had begun a silent review of all the hurts, but now, unexpectedly, those thoughts faded, and a different sort of memory crept into my mind. It was a morning long ago.

I was sitting on our worn green sofa, sulkily watching Mama rush around getting ready for work.

"You're never home," I said accusingly. "You're never here. You don't do anything for us like a real mother. Robin's mother bakes jelly cookies for her lunch box."

"Linda," she said wearily, "I go to work so you can *have* a lunch. I'm so tired when I come home; I have no time for baking."

"You have no time for anything!"

"Would you rather see us go on welfare?" she asked quietly.

I wasn't sure exactly what that meant. "Yes!"

Mama grew pale. "Oh, honey, you think welfare's fun? My mama and I were on welfare once. We never had enough food, or clothes, or money for doctors. I just want you and your sister to have it a little easier. But I can't be everything. I get tired, too."

"Well, in real families," I said spitefully, "the mommy stays home."

She winced, but said lightly, "In this family, I'll get fired if I'm late again," and she ran out to catch the train.

The following week I found three large homemade jelly cookies in my lunch box. But I never thanked Mama, never even mentioned that I'd seen the cookies. How many times, I wondered, had I ignored Mama's efforts to please me?

Now all the little things she'd done came flying to me.

Mama staying up late to restitch my worn-out seams, Mama teaching me how to braid my long dark hair, Mama stepping in when my sister and I had an argument. As badly as I treated her, it was still Mama who had always been there for me. Why hadn't I been able to see this before?

Right there in the car I did what I had seen Mama do so many times — I bowed my head and prayed, silently. My prayer was for forgiveness — but this time for myself. *And please, God, help me to get rid of my bitterness.*

"Greg, I know this is going to sound crazy, but —"

"You want to go back to your mother's," he finished. He was already smiling, turning the car around.

Later, sitting in Mama's familiar, cozy kitchen, I gave silent thanks. I had watched Mama move about this kitchen a thousand times, but I had always been too angry to feel the strength of her love, the steady warmth of her support.

"Mama?" I said hesitantly, not sure how to begin. "Do you think sometime you could show me your recipe for jelly cookies?"

For a moment I thought she wasn't going to answer, but then I realized she was nodding, and in a voice so low I could hardly hear, she whispered, "You remember those cookies after all these years?"

"Yes, Mama," I said, "I remember."

Youth fades, love droops, the leaves of
friendship fall; a mother's secret love
outlives them all.
— OLIVER WENDELL HOLMES

ALWAYS MAMA
CLARA WALLACE NAIL

Grocery and errand day again, and I was on
my way to pick up Mama. I hoped she'd be
ready.

Of late she'd paid scant attention to the
clock. It was frustrating to have to wait for
her. Half the time she wasn't even dressed
when I got to her house. I'd grown impa-
tient with her childlike ways. Not that
she'd ever had a good sense of time, but
now she had grown worse. She was seventy-
nine years old, and somewhere along the
way we seemed to have changed roles. I
had begun to think of her in almost juve-
nile terms.

I drove into her yard, and as I opened
the car door I heard the sound of a horse's

scream. Beyond the house I could see a flurry of activity in the cow pasture, where several handymen were replacing some barbed wire fencing. I headed toward them. And there was Mama — hurrying ahead of me. I called, but she paid no attention. I ran after her, but she didn't slow down.

Now I could see the horse, a bay I didn't recognize, caught in the barbed wire and spooked. His thrashing rear legs kicked at the men. With nostrils flared and hooves pounding, he let out angry squeals. He was a terrified animal, and my elderly mother was headed straight for him. "No, Mama," I thought out loud. "Don't! It's been too long."

In her younger days Mama could handle any horse. My earliest memories are of the smell of leather, the squeak of the saddle, and Mama behind me, supporting me as her horse moved beneath us. Mama's firm hand was on the rein; Mama was in charge.

An old World War I cavalryman who boarded with us in those days said Mama had the light touch. "Only special horse people have the light touch," he told me, "and your mother has it."

Now just as she reached the big stallion,

one of the men tried to stop her. "Miss Nell, get back!" he shouted. "He's a mean 'un. Came running across the field at us."

He was yelling loudly, but I didn't intervene. I was already thinking back to a time when I obeyed whatever Mama said. She put out her arm with a flattened hand, a sign for us to be still. To my surprise, I shook my head at the man as if to say, *It's all right; she can handle it*. At the same time, my mouth was dry as a bone, and I said a quick prayer.

Mama spoke soothing words to the horse. "What's the matter, pretty boy? Let's see about you." She made soft chirping sounds, and her movements were calm and slow, so familiar to me. She put her hand on his thigh, the thigh that moments before had strained with taut muscles to strike out. The trembling stopped. She caressed his flank and patted his neck, speaking endearments all the time. His high-pitched squeal turned to strange little whimpers that sounded like a sobbing child being comforted.

The fencing was caught around his leg. He would have to be backed out. One of the men made a sudden movement to go to Mama's aid. Again I shook my head. The animal's size didn't matter now.

Mama was in control. With soft commands she encouraged him slowly backward.

Then she spoke to us with a sharp order. "Get clean rags, water, and some of that homemade soap." As I turned to obey, she called after me, "And a strip of sheeting." Already she was stanching the flow of blood with her apron.

After receiving the material, she sponged the wound clean and pulled the long tear together. While I held one end of the sheeting, she bound it around the stallion's leg with just the right pressure. "This will hold until a vet can see him," she explained. The rest of us remained silent, marveling at her efficiency.

In that moment, I saw something else. Mama was in command. And I was proud of her. She was the mother figure again and I the progeny. The proper order had been restored. Oh, I knew I would still have to be sure her bills were paid and see that she kept her doctor appointments. But it seemed God was reminding me that despite her childish ways, Mama was still the parent. No matter what else changed as she grew older, she still deserved my honor and respect.

The calmed horse was led away to the stable until we could find its owner. I noticed Mama's hand trembled a little when she patted him on the rump. She looked down at her bloodstained dress.

"Well, I'm not quite ready," she said. "You'll have to wait while I dress."

I put my arm around her as we started for the house. "It's okay, Mama. I don't mind waiting."

Love,
Your Son

She riseth also while it is yet night and giveth meat to her household. Her children rise up and call her blessed.
— PROVERBS 31:15, 28

MAMA'S SOUP POT
LEO BUSCAGLIA

There are too many treasures in life we take for granted, the worth of which we don't fully realize until they're pointed out to us in some unexpected way. So it was with Mama's soup pot.

I can still see it sitting on the stove in all its chipped white-and-blue-enameled glory, its contents bubbling, steam rising as if from an active volcano. When I entered the back porch, the aroma was not only mouth-watering, but reassuring. Whether Mama was standing over the pot stirring with a long wooden spoon or not, I knew I was home.

There was no recipe for her minestrone soup. It was always a work in progress. It had been so since her girlhood in the Piemonte mountains of northern Italy, where she learned its secret from her nonna (grandma), who had inherited it from generations of nonnas.

For our large immigrant family, Mama's soup guaranteed we would never go hungry. It was a simmering symbol of security. Its recipe was created spontaneously from what was in the kitchen. And we could judge the state of our family economy by its contents. A thick brew with tomatoes, pasta, beans, carrots, celery, onion, corn, and meat indicated things were going well with the Buscaglias. A watery soup denoted meager times. And never was food thrown out. That was a sin against God. Everything ended up in the minestrone pot.

Its preparation was sacred to Mama. To her, cooking was a celebration of God's providence. Each potato, each shred of chicken was placed in the pot with grateful thanks. I think of Mama whenever I read Proverbs 31:15, 28: "She riseth also while it is yet night and giveth meat to her household. . . . Her children rise up and call her blessed" (KJV).

At one time, however, Mama's soup pot became a source of embarrassment to me, for I feared it would cost me a new friend I had made at school. Sol was a thin, dark-haired boy, and an unusual pal for me because his father was a doctor and they lived in the best part of town. Often Sol invited me to his home for dinner. The family had a cook in a white uniform who worked in a kitchen of gleaming chrome and shining utensils. Though the food was good, I found it bland without the heartiness of my home fare served from flame-blackened pots. Moreover, the atmosphere matched the food. Everything was so formal. Sol's mother and father were polite, but conversation around the table was stilted and subdued. And no one hugged! The closest I saw Sol get to his father was a handshake.

In our family, warm hugs were a constant — men, women, boys, and girls — and if you didn't kiss your mother, she demanded: "Whatsa matter, you sick?"

But at that time in my life, all this was an embarrassment.

I had known Sol would like to eat dinner at our house, but that was the last thing I wanted. My family was so different. No other kids had such pots on their stoves, nor did they have a mama whose first action upon seeing you enter the house was to sit you down with a spoon and bowl.

"People in America don't do things like that," I tried to convince Mama.

"Well, I'm not people," was her proud retort. "I'm Rosina. Only crazy people don't want my minestrone."

Finally Sol pointedly asked if he could come to our house. I had to say yes. I knew nothing would make Mama happier. But I was in a state of anxiety. Eating with my family would turn Sol off completely, I believed.

"Mama, why can't we have some American food like hamburgers or fried chicken?"

She fixed me with a stony glare and I knew better than to ask again.

The day Sol came over I was a nervous wreck. Mama and the other nine family members welcomed him with embraces and slaps on the back.

Soon we were sitting at the heavy, deeply stained, and ornately carved table that was Papa's pride and joy. It was covered with an ostentatious, bright oilcloth.

And sure enough, after Papa asked the blessing, we were instantly faced with bowls of soup.

"Eh, Sol," Mama asked, "you know what this is?"

"Soup?" Sol responded.

"No soup," Mama said emphatically. "It's *minestrone!*" She launched into a long, animated explanation of the power of minestrone: how it cured colds, headaches, heartaches, indigestion, gout, and liver ailments.

After feeling Sol's muscles, Mama convinced him that the soup would also make him strong, like the Italian-American hero Charles Atlas. I cringed, convinced that this would be the last time I would ever see my friend Sol. He would certainly never return to a home with such eccentric people, odd accents, and strange food.

But to my amazement, Sol politely finished his bowl and then asked for *two more*. "I like it a lot," he said, slurping.

When we were saying our good-byes, Sol confided, "You sure have a great family. I wish my mom could cook that good." Then he added, "Boy, are you lucky!"

Lucky? I wondered as he walked down the street waving and smiling.

Today I know how lucky I was. I know that the glow Sol experienced at our table was much more than the physical and spiritual warmth of Mama's minestrone. It was the unalloyed joy of a family table where the real feast was love.

Mama died a long time ago. Someone turned off the gas under the minestrone pot the day after Mama was buried, and a glorious era passed with the flame. But the godly love and assurance that bubbled amidst its savory ingredients still warms my heart today.

Sol and I continued our friendship through the years. I was best man at his wedding. Not long ago I visited his house for dinner. He hugged all his children and they hugged me. Then his wife brought out steaming bowls of soup. It was chicken soup, thick with vegetables and savory chunks of meat.

"Hey, Leo," Sol asked, "do you know what this is?"

"Soup?" I responded, smiling.

"Soup!" he huffed. "This is *chicken soup!* Cures colds, headaches, indigestion. Good for your liver!" Sol winked.

I felt I was home again.

*Great works do not always lie in our way,
but every moment we may do little ones
excellently, that is, with great love.*
— Saint Francis of Sales

Rocks in My Head
Kathy Johnson Gale

"Look what I bought for you boys at the store today," Mom said proudly. She reached into the sack and pulled out two shiny new lunch boxes.

Oh, no! I thought to myself.

"Cool!" Jason cried, grabbing the one covered with brightly colored pictures of dinosaurs.

Mom said, "I picked this one for you, Eric, because I know how much you like outer space."

She handed me the lunch box decorated with rocket ships and planets. "Thanks, Mom," I managed.

I took the lunch box from her and stared at it. Flicking the latch with my thumb, I

228

opened it up and looked at the chunky Thermos inside, galaxies spinning around it. How could I tell Mom that boys didn't take lunch boxes to school in the fourth grade unless they wanted to be called babies?

I smiled, but couldn't think of anything else to say. Mom had been so sad since the divorce, and she was just starting to be her old self again. I didn't want to say or do anything that would upset her.

I took the lunch box to my room and dropped it on the floor by my bed. I paced around my room a few times, thinking. Then, I picked up a shiny black igneous rock from the top of my bookshelf and started tossing it into the air and catching it.

I had the best rock collection of any kid in school. Mom was always bugging me about it, though. "When are you going to do something about all of these silly rocks, Eric?" she would ask. "I can't even dust your room."

I could see why it bothered her. There were rocks covering just about every surface in my room, including the windowsills. But no way could I part with them. Each one was special. I had several geodes with sparkling crystals inside, a quartz rock that my friend Tommy gave me, fossil rocks that I found at our old house before the divorce, a bunch of agates that my grandpa gave me, and a real moon rock from Dad. At least, he said it was real. I began bouncing the igneous rock against my bed. What was I going to say to Mom? How could I tell her — without hurting her feelings — that I didn't want the lunch box?

By bedtime, I still hadn't thought of a way to tell Mom I didn't want a lunch box. Tomorrow was the first day of school, and my new clothes were laid out on a chair. The lunch box was still beside my bed, eating away at my self-confidence.

I fell back onto my pillow and stared out the window. Moonlight played softly on the rocks along my windowsill. *Only a kid with rocks in his head would carry a lunch box to school,* I thought. And then it hit me. The solution to my problem. It had been right under my nose all along.

Next morning, I found Mom in the kitchen cooking eggs.

"Hey, Mom," I said, holding the lunch box out for her to see. "This lunch box is great; it holds a lot of rocks."

She looked at the lunch box and then at me. "You put rocks in your new lunch box?"

I was talking fast now. "Sure. I can fit in all the ones that were on my windowsills and some from my desk too."

"But what are you going to take your lunch in?"

"I'll just take it in a paper sack," I said, pulling a small sack from the drawer. "That's what most of the guys do, anyway."

A slow smile came to Mom's face. "I see . . . well, hmm." She scooped the eggs onto my plate. "Rocks in your lunch box. Sounds like a good idea . . . especially if you'll wash off those windowsills when you get home." There was a mischievous light in her eyes that I hadn't seen for a long time.

"No problem," I said. And then I hugged her.

A guy would have to have rocks in his head not to love a mom like that.

*A thousand words will not leave so deep
an impression as one deed.*
— Henrik Ibsen

Message of Love
Brad Wilcox

My lonely headlights searched the fresh
snow ahead of me. I fumbled with my top
coat button against the cold. Of all nights for
this to happen! Dad away in Seattle on business, and my brother Roger at college!

"Don't think about it, just drive," I told
myself as the wheels slid sideways on the
icy street. I tried to think of a song to fill
the rhythm of the struggling windshield
wipers. But there was no song in me.

No wonder it had happened. This snow-
storm, the same snowfall I had thought so
beautiful and pure just two hours ago, was
now the white-cloaked villain who had so
mercilessly forced my mother's car off the
road. Now she lay unconscious in critical
condition.

232

"Are you her son?" they had asked on the telephone.

"I'll be right there!" I had shouted.

Dad didn't know, and Rog didn't know. There was just me in my old heap of a Chevy, and this snow.

A frozen string of tears beaded my cheeks. I pulled the glove from my left hand to wipe my eyes.

Just the other day Mom said these gloves were too small, I thought, as I flexed my cold fingers to circulate the blood. *Are the gloves too small, or are my hands too big?* These hands which just a few hours before were squeezed so lovingly by my beautiful mother.

"That snow looks bad, Mom. I wish you weren't going out tonight."

"I do, too. But some things just have to be done." She reached to squeeze my hand good-bye.

"Aw, come on, Mom. I'm too old for that," I declared, withdrawing my hand. "I'm not a little boy. I don't want to play baby games any more."

"It's just my way of telling you, son. It's our secret code."

"I know, I know," I said with exasperated resentment. "I'm tired of your silly secret code. Three squeezes, one-two-three. I love you," I mimicked in full-toned sarcasm. "Never again, Mom."

The words burned in my mind as I stared blankly ahead. I could still see her hurt smile.

Three squeezes had always been our love language. Because of that simple code, countless cuts and bruises had been healed. How often had we sat in church, hand-delivering our secret message, or walked through the park saying, "I love you," in silent communication?

During my sixteen-year lifetime, Mom and Dad must have invested a trillion hours per year just helping me. Ever since I could remember, there had always been thoughtful rewards, and lately, dollar bills for feeding my gas tank or feeding my date. But always delivered with our secret code, the secret code that my hands had, only two hours ago, grown too large to return.

I clutched the steering wheel with one hand. Gripping the old glove in my teeth, I finally managed to fit it back over my chilled fingers. The snow fell lighter now. I was making better time.

I had never faced a problem entirely alone before. Rog had been the dependable big brother who always shepherded me past pitfalls, buying my lunch tickets, picking me up after practice.

I had wanted responsibility, and now I had it! Terrified is a pale word to describe how I felt.

What if she dies! Could anything ever be right again? Suddenly the snow looked sticky and ugly. How I wished I could bury the snow, my head, my hands, responsibility, everything!

The lights of the hospital guided me through the white blackness. My old car chugged, sputtered, and died. With a frustrated shove I freed the frozen door. A slip on the ice sent me sprawling to the frozen pavement. I stood up and shook myself. The biting wind hurried me toward the institutional glass doors.

I stammered Mom's name to the receptionist. It sounded foreign. To me, she was always just "Mom."

The receptionist referred to her files. She seemed slow, but finally faced me. She manipulated the switchboard, then directed me to the elevator.

"A nurse will be waiting on the third floor. I hope everything will be all right."

My rapid steps echoed dully in the endless tunnel of the hospital hallway. Elevator doors closed, trapping me inside, then drew aside again like curtains opening on a stage set. A young nurse entered stage left, taking my arm, including me in the scene.

"Please wait here," she told me. "I'll get the doctor."

I leaned my forehead against the sharp coldness of the window, peering sightlessly into the night. Snow whirled dizzily against the pane.

"Are you her son?"

I turned to find a new character in my drama. Even from my six-foot height the doctor seemed tall. Costumed in surgical green, he was well-cast in his role.

"I'm glad you came so quickly. Since your father is not here, you must be the man of the family."

I shifted uneasily in my wet shoes. Those were the exact words Dad had left with me. I wanted Dad here; here in the hospital where I was born, here with this tall doctor wearing this clinical face.

He led me down the hall. "This is her room. Now remember, son, you mustn't expect her to respond. She may not even recognize you. She is in a semiconscious state and suffering considerable pain."

I pushed the door open and stepped inside. There lay a figure surrounded by machines, strapped and laced with tubes and needles. A transparent oxygen tent encompassed the upper half of the body.

As I stood looking across at that pale, pained face, I realized this was not another character in my dramatic scene. This was my mother!

Mom's eyes opened in an unnatural stare. I stepped across the silence of that small hospital room, reached out, and laid my trembling hand on hers. I knew what I had to do. My message had to be clear. I squeezed — one-two-three. Only God knew how important it was that she understand.

Her eyes flickered. She knew me! A tear ran down my face and dropped upon my hand — the hand that had been too grown-up for this baby game.

My hand enfolded hers and passed our secret code again and again until she fell asleep. Through the window I could see the snow falling gently now.

"Thank you," I prayed in marvelous relief. "Thank you for life, and hands, and secret codes."

*He that sweareth to his own hurt, and
changeth not . . . he that doeth these
things shall never be moved.*
— PSALM 15:4–5

I PROMISED MAMA
NISSAN KRAKINOWSKI

It was in a Nazi concentration camp in
Stutthof, in the Danzig region, that I promised my mother, Pesah, I would look after
my brother, Chaim. Though I was still
young myself, I think Mama saw that I was
the one with chutzpah, already wise to the
ways of the world.

But the world's ways in those awful days
were inspired by the spirit of evil, I believe. In June of 1941 my family had lived
in Kaunas, Lithuania. One day at mid-
night a friend frantically beat on our door
to warn us of what the invading Nazis
would do to us Jews. But Papa, a highly
respected tailor, could not believe him.
My father, Shimon, was one of the first

Jews to be shot in Kaunas.

Mama, Chaim, and I were forced to live in the Kaunas ghetto, and to labor on the local military airport. Mama helped keep us alive. One slice of moldy bread washed down with a watery soup was our only daily meal. She would always break her bread in half and give each of us a quarter.

"Mama, what are you *doing?*" I'd scold.

"Shhhh," she would whisper, looking around. "I don't need so much. It's better you two should have it."

It hurt me to see Mama wasting away, but she would not have had it otherwise.

She reminded me that we do not live by bread alone, but by every word that comes from G- d,* a reference to Deuteronomy 8:3. "Keep your mind on him, my sons, for what the dwellers of Gehenna are trying to do here won't last. Always have faith," she emphasized, "and he will watch over you."

I needed him more than ever that terrible day in 1944 when Chaim and I were herded into a line to be sent to a camp in Kaufering, Bavaria. The Nazis had chosen only those who could work. It was obvious

*A spelling used by the author and many other Jews who, out of reverence, do not write the full word when referring to the Lord.

what would happen to the ones left behind.

We had only a moment to say good-bye. Mama held us close to her bony body, her dark-brown eyes full of tears. Then, as we turned to go, she held me back a moment. "Listen, my son," she whispered, "you should always keep an eye on your brother. I feel if you survive, he will survive. Stay with him always."

"Yes, Mama," I choked.

"Promise?"

"I promise."

That was the last I ever saw of my mother.

When we stumbled out of the boxcar at the new camp, we were so stiff we could hardly walk. A guard began beating me for not moving fast enough. As his truncheon slammed my head, all went black. I regained consciousness, my face in the cold mud, tasting salty blood. I was glad Mama was not in this place.

She would have been overcome on seeing the decline of Chaim, who became more frail every day. He had been bruised on his right leg, making it difficult to walk. Then came the day they lined us all into two columns, facing each other. Those able to work, including me, stood in one formation. Chaim and the rest of the sick ones made up the other. Guards stood ready with rifles. I saw Chaim's eyes filled with fear and tears. Heartsick, I wondered, *Should I run to his line?* Finally, in desperation, I took a terrible chance and motioned Chaim to join me. He suddenly left his line and limped toward me. I held my breath, praying for his safety. Everyone saw, but no one stopped him. They thought, I assumed, someone had given permission. I knew it was a miracle.

Though Chaim remained among us living, he slipped lower. Gangrene had blackened his leg, and he could not walk. I tried to cover for him as much as possible. And the guards were not so strict when rumors circulated that the Allies were approaching. I wished they would obliterate the camp and put us out of our misery.

Then on the morning of April 27, 1945, the Nazi commandant issued a proclamation. All prisoners were to leave the camp at noon to go deeper into Germany, after which the premises would be dynamited to the ground. We knew this was to eliminate evidence of the atrocities.

But what about Chaim and the others who were unable to walk? I worried. By now everyone else was leaving the barracks. I sat with Chaim and looked into his eyes. "Chaim," I pleaded, "you *have* to walk. Look, I can help you."

"No, Nissan," he moaned, "I can't move." His thin hand pressed mine. "Go," he pleaded. "I'll be all right. Go yourself."

The barracks had become quiet as the others were lining up at the gate. Just to be outside this place, no matter where, would be heaven. Thoughts raged within me. *Your mother will never know. Your brother is close to death anyway. Don't be a fool. Go!*

But I also remembered Mama's hand on my arm and her pleading: "Stay with him always."

I promise, Mama.

I leaned down and put my arms around my brother's skeletal body. "No, Chaim. I stay no matter what."

We heard soldiers hurriedly laying dynamite, others stringing wires. At this point I committed us into the arms of G- d.

By noon only a few of us remained in the barracks. A low chanting of prayers began. I joined in with Chaim, praying that death would be quick. . . .

Then, a distant rumble. It came closer, the groaning of tanks. It had to be our liberators. Within an hour American soldiers poured through the gate. The dynamiting never came. Who knows what happened?

The soldiers were so kind, so good-natured. They gave us chocolate bars and food. I ate so much so fast, I became ill. Chaim was given medical treatment and recovered soon after.

Later I learned terrible news. I happened to meet a fellow inmate who had left with the others that April morning. He supported himself on crutches. "We were all walking along the road when fighter planes roared down and strafed us with their machine guns," he said. "It was dusk and they must have thought we were enemy troops." He stared into the distance. "Many were killed." He looked at me and said, "You were very lucky." As he limped slowly away, I thought, *Lucky? No. Obedient.*

Honor thy . . . mother:
that thy days may be long upon the land
which the Lord thy God giveth thee.
— EXODUS 20:12

THE DAY I GREW UP
GREG HUNTER

I know this may sound strange, but at one time in my childhood I was very much ashamed of my mother. Today the shame I feel is for myself, especially since the reason for my attitude toward her was that she was totally deaf.

Deafness swept over my mother when she was just a little girl. Doctors were baffled. They tried their best to help her, but all efforts failed. It is still unknown to this day why she is deaf.

When I was still in grammar school, we were a close-knit family who lived happily in a red-and-white trailer on a grass-covered hill in the country. Yet the time came when I began to see that my mother was different from other mothers, and knowing that she was deaf and had a slight speech impediment embarrassed me. I stopped inviting my friends over to my house, and I avoided being around my mother whenever we were out in public. She noticed this strange behavior in me, but she overlooked it and loved me all the same.

One Saturday afternoon, though, something happened that changed my foolish attitude completely.

My mother and I went shopping for groceries that day, and I did as I always did whenever we went to the supermarket: I waited for my mother to get her cart and begin her shopping, then I headed for the magazine rack to spend my time reading the magazines rather than being around her when she shopped. She tended to be a little loud at times and cause unnecessary scenes. Just the thought of being around her frightened me, because I did not want people to know that she was my mother.

After an hour or so, I finally saw my mother pushing her cartload of groceries to the checkout counter. Knowing that I was safe from embarrassment, I relaxed against the magazine rack. But while the cashier was ringing up the total of the groceries, my mother suddenly could not find her purse. Her eyes widened, her mouth dropped, and she started yelling with her high-pitched voice that she had lost her purse. People turned their heads, staring at her, thinking she was crazy or something. My face turned pale and my body froze in fear that she might call for me.

As my grief-stricken mother stood alone in desperation before all of those people, she looked about, asking people in her squeaky voice if they had seen her small purse. When no one answered her, she began to cry and started to lose control of herself. I remained silent behind the magazine stand, looking anxiously for an escape route out of the store, but there was none.

Suddenly I heard her cry out my name. I wanted to run and hide, but my body would not budge. My mind raced and my thoughts were spinning and becoming more confused; but like a selfish fool, I remained frozen. I slowly turned to gaze at my mother, and I saw her crying more as she searched frantically for her purse. A man tried to calm her down, but she only yelled out, screaming that someone must have stolen her purse. The man kept asking her what was wrong, and she kept repeating that her purse was gone. But he could not understand her.

Suddenly, my heart began to go out to her. I really couldn't figure out what was happening with my feelings, but finally I seemed to realize how uncaring and selfish I had been. I knew I had to drop the ignorant attitude I had carried with me for so long and run to my mother with outstretched arms to prove to her that I did indeed love her and would protect her.

As I raced toward her, I thanked God for helping me see my mistake, and I reached out for the most special person in my life and held her with all my might. Then as my embarrassment faded away, I became aware of something unique and wonderful. This lady who held me in her loving arms was the caring lady who gave birth to me, raised me to be a good person, raised my sister and my four brothers to be good and responsible people, took care of all of us when we were sick, was always there when we needed her, and, most of all, loved her family more than she did her own life. All of this is what made her special.

When the crowd of people finally receded and my mother took control of herself, we found her purse behind a box of cereal in the grocery cart. We both laughed hysterically, happy that this day had brought us closer together.

On our way home, I thought deeply about why my mother seemed unhappy at times. I knew that, deep down in her heart, she longed to hear again. She prayed so hard, wanting to be able to hear the wonderful world and hear, for the first time, her own children's voices. But only God knows what is best for her.

I am thankful for the Lord's help in that weekend incident that occurred so many years ago. I am proud of this courageous woman, my mother, my love.

The angels whispering to one another can find among their . . . terms of love none so devotional as that of "Mother."
— EDGAR ALLAN POE

ON J. A. M. WHISTLER
AUTHOR UNKNOWN

In 1878, in the little essay he called "The Red Rag," he would write: "Art should be independent of all claptrap — should stand alone, and appeal to the artistic sense of eye or ear without confounding this with emotions entirely foreign to it, as devotion, pity, love, patriotism, and the like. . . . Take the picture of my mother, exhibited at the Royal Academy as an *Arrangement in Grey and Black*. Now that is what it is. To me it is interesting as a picture of my mother; but what can or ought the public to care about the identity of the portrait?" Yet at a slightly later date, in a private conversation and with just a hint of his usual air of listening to his own phrases, he himself came close to taking the

249

side of "claptrap," and an alert friend noted the betrayal with relish: ". . . we were looking at the *Mother*. I said some string of words about the beauty of the face and figure, and for some moments Jimmy looked and looked, but he said nothing. His hand was playing with that tuft upon his nether lip. It was, perhaps, two minutes before he spoke. 'Yes,' very slowly, and very softly — 'yes, one does like to make one's mummy just as nice as possible.' "

*The future destiny of the child
is always the work of the mother.*
— Napoleon Bonaparte

Mothers,
You Are Great!
Charles Swindoll

I know of no more permanent imprint on a life than the one made by mothers. I guess that's why Mother's Day always leaves me a little nostalgic. Not simply because my mother has gone on (and heaven's probably cleaner because of it!), but because that's the one day the real heroines of our world get the credit they deserve. Hats off to every one of you!

More than any statesman or teacher, more than any minister or physician, more than any film star, athlete, business person, author, scientist, civic leader, entertainer, or military hero . . . you are the most influential person in your child's life.

Never doubt that fact!

Not even when the dishes in the sink resemble the Leaning Tower . . . or the washing machine gets choked and dies . . . or the place looks a wreck and nobody at home stops to say, "Thanks Mom. You're great."

It's still worth it. You are great. This is your time to make the most significant contribution in all of life. Don't sell it short. In only a few years it will all be a memory. Make it a good one.

Remembering Grandmother

A gracious woman retains honor.
— PROVERBS 11:26

BUBBA
BERT CLOMPUS

I was about five when I first realized that Bubba — Yiddish for "grandmother" — was not on good terms with Mom. Whenever Dad drove us to Harrisburg, Pennsylvania, to visit his mother, it was always the same story. If Bubba spoke to Mom at all, her words were clipped and cold. Then on one visit, Mom and Bubba were washing the dinner dishes when a teacup slipped out of Mom's hands and shattered on the floor. A look of disdain clouded Bubba's broad face. "Mollie," she grumbled, "you never were good enough for my son!"

I was shocked. How could Bubba talk like that? My eyes welled with tears as I watched Mom bite her lip and look to Dad. He was red-faced and wordless; but my grandfather's eyes blazed at Bubba.

"You apologize to Mollie!" Grandfather demanded. Bubba, a large woman who dwarfed my short and wiry grandfather, merely folded her arms and pursed her lips stubbornly.

Our visit ended abruptly, but not before my grandfather steered me down the steps of the small apartment to his grocery store below. He slid open the door at the back of the candy case. "Here, Bert, take one," he said, as if the sweetness could purge the bitter aftertaste of Bubba's outburst. I shook my head, then relented, selecting a cherry sour ball.

I was still rolling it around in my mouth and resisting the urge to bite into it as we drove home. Mom must have been doing the same thing with Bubba's words, rolling them around in her mind and fighting the urge to complain to Dad. About the time I finally crunched the sour ball, Mom blurted out, "Ike, why didn't you say something?"

Dad didn't answer. He only gripped the steering wheel a little tighter and drove a little faster. At last Mom cried out, "So is that what you think too? I'm not good enough?"

I was nearly thrown off the backseat as Dad slammed on the brake pedal and swerved to a stop on the shoulder of the road. "How can you say that, Mollie?" he gasped, grabbing her hand.

"I know I had only a third-grade education when I came to this country," Mom sobbed. "I know I had to sew in a sweatshop to help support my family. I know you are your mother's favorite son. But does that make me not good enough, Ike?"

My father's face, usually so stern, softened. "Are you through?" he asked quietly. Mom nodded, rummaging in her pocketbook for a tissue. Their eyes finally met, and Dad kissed his fingertips and touched them softly to Mom's lips. I knew things were all right again. But I also knew how Dad felt, torn between the two women he loved most in the world, not wanting to hurt either one.

The next time we went to Harrisburg, Mom insisted on waiting in the car while we visited with Bubba.

"I'm staying with Mom," I declared loyally.

"Go with your father, Bert," Mom ordered.

"All right," I said, giving in, "but I'm not speaking to Bubba."

Bubba pretended to be disappointed that Mom wasn't with us. When she smiled and spread her huge arms wide for me, my resolve evaporated. I melted, all the while feeling like a traitor. But what five-year-old can resist a grandmother's hug? When Dad and my grandfather went downstairs to the store, I mustered my courage and asked Bubba why she didn't love Mom. She refused to answer.

"But you love me, don't you?" I persisted.

Bubba pulled me onto her lap. "Sure I do!" she said fiercely.

"Well, if you love me, why can't you be nice to Mom?"

Bubba shrugged. "It's different," she said, "and you're too young to understand." Just then Dad came upstairs and said it was time to leave.

Not long after, Bubba took ill with a severe case of the flu. Stubborn as always, she refused to go to the hospital or stay with any of her children nearby. My grandfather had his hands full working twelve-hour days tending the store, so my dad offered to bring Bubba to recuperate with us, in the home of her favorite son. To my surprise, Mom agreed. My stomach knotted at the prospect of the two of them under one roof.

The next day Dad followed Bubba into

the house, carrying a battered brown valise and a large paper bag. He put the bag on the kitchen table. "What's this?" Mom asked.

"I brought my own food," said Bubba, punctuating her statement with a series of hacking coughs.

Mom emptied the bag of its contents: a large jar of pickles, another of sauerkraut, and six cans of store-bought chicken soup. "This isn't food for a sick person," Mom said, glancing dismissively at Bubba. The tension between them made my knees weak. *Lord,* I prayed desperately, *please let them get along just this once. Please.*

"I'll get Bubba settled in the guest room," Dad interjected quickly, taking my grandmother by the arm.

"She's not eating *this* food, Ike!" Mom called after them.

"I will too!" Bubba coughed.

"I don't want her dying in my house!"

"I wouldn't dream of it, Mollie!"

"Both of you — that's enough!" Dad shouted, pulling Bubba up the stairs. When he returned, he took Mom aside. "You've got to try to show my mother respect while she's in this house," he whispered hoarsely. Then he stomped off to work.

Red-faced and silent, muttering a prayer, Mom swept aside Bubba's groceries and went to work herself — chopping and slicing, preparing a big pot of her home-made chicken soup. While the glorious concoction bubbled and simmered on the stove, Mom baked a fresh loaf of challah — the sweet braided bread she usually made for the Sabbath. When it was all done, she fixed a tray with her best china and carried it up to Bubba. There was something almost defiant about her as she climbed the stairs.

I tiptoed behind and watched Mom silently hand Bubba the tray. There was a long nerve-racking pause before Bubba croaked, "For me?" Mom didn't answer. Instead she briskly smoothed the covers on Bubba's bed and left.

Downstairs I asked Mom why she had gone to such trouble for Bubba. "I thought challah and soup was just for Fridays? I mean, Bubba isn't even nice to you."

"That doesn't matter, Bert," she said. "She's still your father's mother and she's still my guest. That's how we'll treat her; that's what God wants."

Later I went up to get Bubba's dishes. "Isn't Mom's chicken soup the best?" I asked her.

Bubba hemmed and hawed and shifted in bed. "It's not half bad," she finally admitted, as if the words were torture to get out.

"Mom," I said, handing her the tray downstairs, "Bubba said your chicken soup is the best."

"She did?" Mom said, failing to mask her surprise. This was high praise coming from Bubba, and I thought Mom straightened a little bit with pride.

Every day, from then on, Mom made Bubba soup and fresh challah, and served it on her best dishes. It was good medicine, and not just for Bubba's flu. Each time Mom took Bubba her tray, they lingered together a little longer. One afternoon, while I listened outside the door, I heard Bubba say, "Mollie, I have six daughters and not one of them makes chicken soup to match yours."

"Oh, go on, Bubba," said Mom modestly. "Can I get you some more?" I peeked into the room just in time to see Bubba raise herself from bed and give Mom a good long hug. I knew how that felt.

Mom was blushing when she came out and scooted me away. But later she took me by the shoulders and said, "Bert, if I grumble about the girl you marry, just tell her to keep trying to love me anyway. God will do the rest."

I think Bubba stayed on a few days extra just because she was having a good time. Seeing his wife and mother get along at last lifted a huge burden from my father. And I was glad God had heard my prayer and helped bring Mom and Bubba together. If we treat one another with respect and love, even if it's difficult, he'll look after the rest. That's what the two women I loved most in the world taught me when I was five years old.

*A good heart is better
than all the heads in the world.*
— EDWARD BULWER-LYTTON

KLEIN GRANDMA
MARILYN KRATZ

We called her "Klein Grandma" — German for "little grandma" — because she was barely five feet tall. She has been gone for over twenty-five years now, but I still miss her in many ways.

I miss the security of her unconditional love. She always had time for me and made me feel special. And of course, I miss her wonderful cooking. In fact, many of my happiest childhood memories are focused around the big oval table in her sunny, lace-curtained dining room. . . .

Grandma loved to begin a big family meal with what seemed, in my little girl eyes, to be a "vat" of homemade chicken noodle soup. That would be followed by hearty main dishes; never fancy, but always satisfying. And then there came dessert! Her unforgettable sour cream cookies were huge — topped with brown sugar icing. After Klein Grandma died, I asked to see her recipe file so I could copy the recipe for those cookies, but it could not be found. I suspect she kept it in her head and never wrote it down.

My dear Klein Grandma was never rich or famous, but she left me the treasured memories of happy hours in her home, where she was always ready to share her love, or a cookie or two. The "flavor" she added to my life made us both richer in a special way. And even though we called her Klein Grandma, she will always be a big part of my life.

*The difference between the impossible and
the possible lies in a man's determination.*
— TOMMY LASORDA

"DON'T THINK IT.
DON'T SAY IT."
JACKIE CLEMENTS-MARENDA

"Oh, Grandma," I wailed, "I can't!" I was seven years old, learning to sew under the patient tutelage of my Grandma Josie. No matter how hard I tried, I ended up with knots and needle pricked thumbs.

"*Can't* is a word this family doesn't know," Grandma told me. "*Can't* is used only by cowards, lazy people, and those who don't know God. You do not fall into any of these categories. Remember, Jacquelyn, with God nothing is impossible."

Her mother had taught her to sew, and Grandma Josie was determined to pass the skill on to me. In spite of my ineptitude, she always smiled and showed me once more how to make the intricate stitches. I loved watching Grandma's needle glide through the white material of the dress she was sewing for my First Communion. Although she was eighty and weakened by a heart condition, she refused to allow her only granddaughter to walk down the church aisle in a store-bought dress and veil.

After a month of daily practice, I hoped Grandma Josie would give up on me. But she didn't, and one day she placed a small muslin-wrapped package in my hands. Inside were the last remnants of the family heirloom lace.

The lace was the only possession my great-grandmother Mary Mahoney brought with her from Ireland when she came to America as a young girl in the mid 1800s. Pieces of it had enhanced every bridal and communion veil worn in our clan from then on. It was the special task of the person to whom it was presented to sew on the lace.

There was so little of it left, and the pieces were so fine they would probably unravel in my hands. Worse still, I was afraid I would mutilate them with my clumsy stitches. "Don't think it. Don't say it," Grandma Josie warned, already sensing what I was about to tell her.

I decided to try another approach. "I don't need the lace, Grandma," I said, avoiding even touching it. "The veil is already beautiful enough."

Grandma Josie's eyes twinkled, but she kept her voice stern. "Wearing the lace is a sign to your family that you have the stamina to become the best woman you can be. My mother was fourteen when the great famine swept through Ireland," she said. "Hundreds of thousands were dying, and her family knew it was only a matter of time before they too starved to death. There was only enough money to send one person to America."

"I'm sure young Mary Mahoney was terrified to board that ship alone, but she didn't tell her parents 'I can't.' She did what she had to do," Grandma explained. "When I lost two of my children to influenza the same year I lost three siblings to tuberculosis, did I neglect the healthy family I had left while I learned to live with my grief? No."

She took me in her arms, hugging me tightly. "If you don't try to put the lace on your veil because you fear the hard work, how will you stand strong against the difficult tasks that wait in your future?"

How I struggled with that lace from then on, often in tears when what I thought I had sewn straight proved to be crooked. But I didn't give up.

Ten days before my Communion, Grandma Josie suffered a stroke and had to be hospitalized. She returned home the day before the ceremony.

"I'm sorry you're sick, Grandma," I whispered, snuggled up next to her in bed. "Please, don't be mad. I couldn't finish putting the lace on my veil. I tried, but I got myself into such a thread knot, I didn't know what to do."

She kissed me. "Don't you worry," she said, and touched my cheek with her right hand, which had been paralyzed into a fist by the stroke. "You tried your best. Now just leave your veil on the chair. We'll finish it for you."

I left the room with tears in my eyes. *Who is "we"?* I wondered.

The morning dawned brightly, but there was no joy in my heart.

I was a failure. I tried to sneak past Grandma's room, but she heard my steps in the hall and called me in.

"You'd better get a move on if you plan to be on time," she said. I was surprised to find her dressed and sitting in a chair. "We got the veil done. Now it's up to you."

My veil lay in her lap. I picked it up and ran my fingers over the delicate stitches that held the precious lace in place. It seemed impossible, but the veil was complete. How had Grandma maneuvered the needle with her twisted right hand?

As usual, she answered my thought: "When you do your best and try your hardest, God's angels fill in the rest."

Thirty-five years later, I am a competent seamstress. But most important, I live by the tradition of Grandma Josie and those who have worn the Irish lace. When I am confronted with a task so difficult it seems insurmountable, I "Don't think it. Don't say it," but do my best and ask God to send his fill-ins.

Living one day in the Spirit is worth more than a thousand lived in the flesh.
— RICHARD OWEN ROBERTS

LET THE HEAT DO THE WORK

KATHIE KANIA

I was a young teen thoroughly uninterested in house chores. The ironing board wobbled and groaned as I drove the iron into the shirt collar one more time. It crinkled even more.

"Your trouble is that you're working too hard," Grandma said, taking the iron. "You let the heat do the work, not all that pushing and pressing." Almost effortlessly, she ironed the collar smooth.

That happened a long time ago, but I thought of it again on a recent hectic day. By afternoon, stress weighed heavily upon me.

Suddenly I could see Grandma taking the iron: "All that pushing and pressing!" I should be letting the Holy Spirit do the work! Wasn't that what "casting all your care upon Him" (1 Peter 5:7) was about?

Sure enough, as I made time to pray for help, I found that the still small Voice was present. Before I knew it, my day's work was done, and I even had time to relax that evening with my family.

Are you working too hard today? Remember Grandma's words: "Let the heat do the work."

Of Mother
& Home

Little keys can open big locks.
Simple words can express great thoughts.
— WILLIAM ARTHUR WARD

MAMA'S DREAM
BETTY MCFARLANE

I wish now that I hadn't opened the old cedar chest, for there, under the quilt I'd come for, was the old familiar box with the words "Acceptance Letters" penciled on it. Memories rushed in and a sense of sadness filled me. Her dream had never become a reality.

Yet as long as I can remember, Mama had always wanted to be a writer. She frequently told us children of the stories she was going to write and where she was going to send them. Most often she would carry a small notebook and, as she hurriedly went her busy way, she would quickly take the notebook out and jot down an idea or two as it came to her.

I first knew Mama was really serious

about her writing twenty years or so ago. She sat at the kitchen table with a tear snaking down her cheek as she put on paper how she had just been forced to sell a horse, an old paint, that she loved. We had needed the money for a house payment.

Mama never sent the article anywhere, but after that day I saw a new light in her eyes. "Children," she told us, "your mama is going to be a writer. I feel that the Lord wants me to write stories that others may read so that they might feel encouraged or uplifted or loved." And this time she put her words into action.

First she took a little of our much-needed money and bought stationery and business cards with her name, address, and the words "Writer and Lecturer" on them. She said it was important to handle things in a businesslike manner; that editors would be more likely to read her work if the cover letter looked proper.

She then cleared a corner in the basement, made a desk by putting a door across two file cabinets, and borrowed an old typewriter from Grandpa. What I really remember most was the box that she carefully placed on the desk with her stationery. It had been covered with cream-colored cotton strewn with blue forget-me-nots. She had tied it with a pale blue ribbon and confidently marked it, "Acceptance Letters." I guess it never occurred to her that she might get some rejections.

Mama gathered her notes, got a copy of the *Writer's Market*, and began writing. However, before she had finished even one article, Dad had left us. Mama was now responsible for the care of her children. With six of us still at home, she spent long hours teaching school, keeping up our home, and guiding us. She always found time to write an encouraging note to be found in our lunch box or on our dresser — but never enough time to write her stories. Mama always told us, "Don't worry about my writing, darlings. God gave me the dream, and he will bring the dream to fulfillment."

Years came and went. I don't recall when Mama put the box away, but I do recall that one day it was no longer on the desk. When I questioned Mama, she only said, "Perhaps someday soon God will give me the time to write stories, but for now, honey, I need to write a letter to your brother."

Occasionally, when I'd see her sitting at her desk, I'd think, *Praise the Lord! Now she is writing her stories.* But instead it was always a letter to one of my brothers in the service, a card to a friend, or a cheerful note to Grandpa.

As we children grew up and began to leave home, Mama would comment that she would soon have the time to write; but then something would always come up — Grandpa got sick and came to live with us; a pregnant teenager needed help; a neighbor had no one but Mama to turn to.

In her mind and on scraps of paper, Mama's stories were born, but Mama never had an article published, for she never had a chance to write.

Now I reached down into the cedar chest and picked up the box. To my surprise, it was very heavy. Its ribbon was worn from tying and untying.

"What could she possibly have kept in here?" I mused aloud. Carefully I opened it. I began to read the "acceptance letters" that lay inside.

"Thank you, Mom, for your daily letters. I could never have made it through boot camp without them."

"Just a note to tell you how much my sister appreciated your support in the many letters you sent her during her years of illness."

"My year in prison would have been unbearable without your letters of hope."

"I was so lonely being away from home for the first time, but your stories of Jesus have kept me happy and unafraid."

"Thank you for taking the time to send me the pretty note cards. Sometimes an old man like me feels like no one wants to bother with him."

"Your letter came when I was at my lowest point. You dared me to be my best, and I am now one of the top salesmen in my organization."

"Mama, your letters have helped me retain my sanity during this difficult time. Thank you for the constant support, concern, hope, and, most of all, love."

God does fulfill people's dreams. Mama *was* a writer.

The hand that rocks the cradle
is the hand that rules the world.
— WILLIAM R. WALLACE

MY MOTHER'S HANDS
CARRIE M. ADAMSON

I can't remember when first I saw my mother's hands. Perhaps it was my first day of school. I clung to her hand that day, as she walked with me to school, and I was most reluctant to part with the security her hand represented.

It could have been the winter I was ten, when her cool, competent hands gently nursed me through a bout with scarlet fever. Perhaps it was the day her deft fingers gave me a final fitting in the formal she had made for the senior prom . . . or the morning of my wedding day, when I came upon her tenderly pressing my bridal veil.

I don't remember when I first *really* saw my mother's hands, but certainly it must have been when she was bestowing largess! They're gentle hands, and tender . . . unadorned except for the thin gold wedding band she has worn for almost half a century. They're small, but can move mountains; they're graceful, but not strangers to hard work. In age, they're resigned. In prayer, they're at peace. In need, they're resourceful. In sickness, they're comfort.

No, I don't remember when I first saw my mother's hands, but I need only close my eyes to see them now . . . and they're a symbol of all that's reassuring and right in the world.

Let us take care of the children,
for they have a long way to go.
— AFRICAN PRAYER

MY MOTHER'S GIFT
SUZANNE CHAZIN

I grew up in a small town where the elementary school was a ten-minute walk from my house and in an age when children could go home for lunch and find their mothers waiting.

At the time, I did not consider this a luxury, although today it certainly would be. I took it for granted that mothers were the sandwich-makers, the finger-painting appreciators, and the homework monitors. I never questioned that this ambitious, intelligent woman, who had had a career before I was born and would eventually return to a career, would spend almost every lunch hour throughout my elementary school years just with me.

I only knew that when the noon bell

rang, I would race breathlessly home. My mother would be standing at the top of the stairs, smiling down at me with a look that suggested I was the only important thing she had on her mind. For this, I am forever grateful.

One lunchtime when I was in the third grade will stay with me always. I had been picked to be the princess in the school play, and for weeks my mother had painstakingly rehearsed my lines with me. But no matter how easily I delivered them at home, as soon as I stepped onstage, every word disappeared from my head.

Finally, my teacher took me aside. She explained that she had written a narrator's part to the play, and asked me to switch roles. Her words, kindly delivered, still stung, especially when I saw my part go to another girl.

I didn't tell my mother what had happened when I went home for lunch that day. But she sensed my unease, and instead of suggesting we practice my lines, she asked if I wanted to walk in the yard. It was a lovely spring day, and the rose vine on the trellis was turning green. Under the huge elm trees, we could see yellow dandelions popping through the grass in bunches, as if a painter had touched our landscape with dabs of gold.

I watched my mother casually bend down by one of the clumps. "I think I'm going to dig up all these weeds," she said, yanking a blossom up by its roots. "From now on, we'll have only roses in this garden."

"But I like dandelions," I protested. "All flowers are beautiful — even dandelions."

My mother looked at me seriously. "Yes, every flower gives pleasure in its own way, doesn't it?" she asked thoughtfully. I nodded, pleased that I had won her over. "And that is true of people too," she added. "Not everyone can be a princess, but there is no shame in that."

Relieved that she had guessed my pain, I started to cry as I told her what had happened. She listened and smiled reassuringly.

"But you will be a beautiful narrator," she said, reminding me of how much I loved to read stories aloud to her. "The narrator's part is every bit as important as the part of a princess."

Over the next few weeks, with her constant encouragement, I learned to take pride in the role. Lunchtimes were spent reading over my lines and talking about what I would wear.

Backstage the night of the performance, I felt nervous. A few minutes before the play, my teacher came over to me. "Your mother asked me to give this to you," she said, handing me a dandelion. Its edges were already beginning to curl and it flopped lazily from its stem. But just looking at it, knowing my mother was out there and thinking of our lunchtime talk, made me proud.

After the play, I took home the flower I had stuffed in the apron of my costume. My mother pressed it between two sheets of paper toweling in a dictionary, laughing as she did it that we were perhaps the only people who would press such a sorry-looking weed.

I often look back on our lunchtimes together. They were the commas in my childhood, the pauses that told me life is not savored in premeasured increments, but in the sum of daily rituals and pleasures we share with loved ones.

A few months ago, my mother came to visit. I took off a day from work and treated her to lunch. The restaurant bustled with noontime activity as business people made deals and glanced at their watches. In the middle of all this sat my mother, now retired, and I. From her face I could see that she relished the pace of the work world. "Mom, you must have been terribly bored staying at home when I was a child," I said.

"Bored? Housework is boring. But you were never boring."

I didn't believe her. "Surely children are not as stimulating as a career."

"A career is stimulating," she said. "I'm glad I had one. But a career is like an open balloon. It remains inflated only as long as you keep pumping. A child is a seed. You water it. You care for it the best you can. And then it grows all by itself into a beautiful flower."

Just then, looking at her, I could picture us sitting at her kitchen table once again, and I understood why I kept that flaky brown dandelion in our old family dictionary pressed between two crumpled bits of paper towel.

Actions speak louder than words.
— Ancient Proverb

My Mother's Desk
Elizabeth Sherrill

I'm sitting at my mother's desk, a mahogany secretary with a writing leaf that folds down to reveal rows of cubbyholes and tiny drawers — even a sliding secret compartment. I've loved it since I was just tall enough to see above the leaf as Mother sat doing letters. Standing by her chair, staring at the ink bottle, pens, and smooth white paper, I decided that the act of writing must be the most delightful thing in the world.

Years later, during her final illness, Mother reserved various items for my sister and brother. "But the desk," she'd repeat, "is for Elizabeth." I sensed Mother communicating with this gift, a communication I'd craved for fifty years.

My mother was brought up in the Victorian belief that emotions were private. Nice people said only nice things. I never saw her angry, never saw her cry. I knew she loved me; she expressed it in action. But as a teenager I yearned for heart-to-heart talks between mother and daughter.

They never happened. And a gulf opened between us. I was "too emotional." She lived "on the surface." She was willing to accept the relationship on these terms. I was not.

As years passed and I raised my own family, I loved the equilibrium Mother's visits brought to our home, her sense of humor, the way she sat at the piano and filled the house with music. But still I kept trying to draw from her what she could not give, a sharing of the deep places of her heart.

At last I set my feelings down on paper. Only one page, the letter took all day to write. I told Mother I loved her and thanked her for our harmonious home. Forgive me, I wrote, for having been critical. In careful words, I asked her to let me know in any way she chose that she did forgive me.

I mailed the letter and waited eagerly for her reply. None came.

Eagerness turned to disappointment, then resignation, and, finally, peace. I couldn't be sure that the letter had even gotten to Mother. I only knew that having written it, I could stop trying to make her into someone she was not. For the last fifteen years of her life we enjoyed a relationship on her terms — light, affectionate, cheerful.

Now the gift of her desk told me, as she'd never been able to, that she was pleased that writing was my chosen work.

My sister stored the desk until we could pick it up. Then it stayed in our attic for nearly a year while we converted a bedroom into a study.

When at last I brought the desk down, it was dusty from months of storage. Lovingly, I polished the drawers and cubbyholes. Pulling out the secret compartment, I found papers inside. A photograph of my father. Family wedding announcements. And a one-page letter, folded and refolded many times.

Send me a reply, my letter asks, in any way you choose. Mother, you always chose the act that speaks louder than words.

Memory is the diary
that we all carry about with us.
— Oscar Wilde

Family Memories
Marjorie Holmes

This past year, when scattered children and grandchildren came home, my oldest son produced a special treat: our old movies of Christmases past, which he'd transferred to videotape.

Laughing and pointing, we sat reliving the merry commotion: hanging up stockings; trimming the tree; rescuing the cat from its tangle of tinsel; church pageants and plays; little angels singing; bathrobed shepherds as they marched onstage.

When the show was over, they all began to discuss other Christmases. "Remember the years we adopted a poor family? You and Daddy let us pick out the turkey, and we were so proud, but one time Mallory dropped it in the mud.

Sure wish we had a shot of that!"

On and on they went, recalling things I'd almost forgotten. And listening, I suddenly noticed: not once did they mention anything they got. Instead, to my surprise, the memories they treasured most were the fun they had in giving.

"Oh, Mother," Melanie was laughing, "doing things like that was the best part of Christmas." The others agreed, expressing only one regret: How nice it would be now to see movies of those times, too.

Then several of them expressed it: Yes, but we didn't need them. The pictures were already engraved on our hearts.

MY WILD IRISH MOTHER

JEAN KERR

I'm never going to write my autobiography, and it's all my mother's fault. I don't hate her, so I have practically no material. In fact, the situation is worse than I'm pretending. We are crazy about her — and you know I'll never get a book out of that.

Mother was born Kitty O'Neill, in Kinsale, Ireland, with bright red hair, bright blue eyes, and the firm conviction that it was wrong to wait for an elevator if you were only going up to the fifth floor. It's not just that she won't wait for elevators; I have known her to reproach herself for missing one section of a revolving door.

Once, when we missed a train from New

York to Washington, I fully expected her to pick up our suitcases and announce, "Well, darling, the exercise will be good for us." When I have occasion to mutter about the financial problems involved in maintaining six children in a large house, Mother is quick to get to the root of the problem. "Remember," she says, "you take cabs a lot." In Mother's opinion, an able-bodied woman is perfectly justified in taking a taxi to the hospital if her labor pains are closer than ten minutes apart. . . .

To her four children — all low-metabolism types, inexplicably — Mother's energy has always seemed awesome. "What do you think?" she's prone to say. "Do I have time to cut the grass before I stuff the turkey?" But her whirlwind activity is potentially less dangerous than her occasional moment of repose. Then she sits, staring into space, clearly lost in languorous memories. The fugitive smile that hovers about her lips suggests the gentle melancholy of one hearing Mozart played beautifully. Suddenly she leaps to her feet. "I know it will work," she says. "All we have to do is to remove that wall, plug up the windows, and extend the porch." . . .

Mother's credo, by the way, is that if you want something, anything, just don't sit there — pray for it. And she combines a Job-like patience in the face of the mysterious ways of the Almighty with a flash of Irish rebellion which will bring her to say — and I'm sure she speaks for many of us — "Jean, what I am really looking for is a blessing that's not in disguise."

She has a knack of penetrating disguises, whether it be small boys who claim they have taken baths or middle-aged daughters who swear they have lost five pounds. She also has a way of cutting things to size. Some time ago I had a collection of short pieces brought out in book form, and I sent one of the first copies to her. "Darling," she wrote, "isn't it marvelous the way those old pieces of yours finally came to the surface like a dead body!"

*Friendship is the only cement that will
ever hold the world together.*
— WOODROW WILSON

MY BEST FRIEND
ELIZABETH DOLE

Mother is my best friend. She has been front and center in my life every step of the way. When I was a young girl, she was there to urge me to do my best. . . . And when the little scrapes and defeats of childhood occurred, Mother was there to turn my sorrows into smiles. . . .

One of the most vivid memories I have of her is on her knees, praying for me, others, and the needs of the world. When I go home to visit, I sleep in the same room with her because we love to talk to each other until we fall asleep.

Mother is unselfish, constantly thinking of others. She endears herself to people because she genuinely cares about every person who crosses her path.

In all matters, before beginning,
a diligent preparation should be made.
— CICERO

MOTHER PREPARES FOR REVIVAL SUNDAY

EDNA LEWIS

Although I didn't think about it at the time, I wonder how my mother made it each year to Revival Sunday, with so much to do and without ever varying from the calm and quiet manner that was her nature. During the week leading up to second Sunday, as well as doing her regular household chores and caring for her brood of chickens, guinea hens, turkeys, and ducks, and her own vegetable garden, she would cut out and sew new dresses of white muslin for the six of us and our two adopted cousins as well as for herself, usually finishing the last buttonholes and sashes late Saturday night in between the cooking that she would have begun for the next day's noontime dinner at the church. . . .

My mother never started her cooking until late on the eve of Revival Sunday. By this time she would have everything gathered in and laid out that she would need, and, I guess, a carefully planned schedule laid out in her mind as well. When we were bathed and turned into bed, no pies or cakes had yet been made. But when we came hurrying down on Sunday morning, the long, rectangular dining-room table would be covered with cakes ready to be iced and pie dishes lined with pastry dough to be filled and baked.

A merry heart doeth good like a medicine:
but a broken spirit drieth up the bones.
— PROVERBS 17:22

MOTHER'S GOOD HUMOR
JEANMARIE COOGAN

My mother was a great handicap to me when I was little. She was different. I learned this very early, when I first began going to other children's houses. There, when the mother opened the door, she said something sensible, like "Wipe your feet" or "You're not bringing that junk in here."

At our house, however, when you rang the bell, the letter slot would open, and a little high voice would pipe out, "I'm the chief troll here. Is that you, Billy Goat Gruff?" Or a syrupy falsetto would sing the first few lines of "Barnacle Bill the Sailor": "Who's that knocking at my door?"

Other times the door would open a slit and my mother, crouched down to our eye level, would say, "I'm the new little girl here. Wait a minute, I'll call my mother." Then the door would close for a second, reopen, and there would be my mother — regular size. "Oh, hello, girls," she'd say. "I didn't know you were there."

In that awful first moment when my new friend would turn to me with a "what kind of place is this" look, I knew how it felt to open a closet and have the family skeleton sprawl all over you. "Mo-*ther*," I would bawl, but my mother would never admit to being the little girl who had opened the door. "You girls are kidding me," she'd say. We'd wind up protesting that a little girl *had* opened the door, when what we really meant was that *no* little girl had opened the door.

It was all very confusing. And different. That was the hard part. She was different from other mothers.

Like the seal in the basement. When we were outside while my mother was washing or ironing in the basement, we would often hear a cheerful barking coming from down there. Mother's explanation was that it was our seal. Every Friday, she made a great show of unwrapping the fish (which eventually wound up on the dinner table) for the seal. And though kids made countless dashes down to the basement trying to catch the creature, he had always "just gone for a ride in the bakery truck" or "was taking his swimming lesson at the Y."

This seal was smart and would answer questions by barking once for "yes" and twice for "no." His reputation soon spread. Children came from blocks around to ask the seal questions at our basement window. The seal was always good for a few barks.

I was mortified to be pointed out as the girl with the seal, but my mother was equal to the occasion. Often when a crowd of little boys huddled at our window, waiting for a bark, my mother would open the door and call out gaily, "Hello, little girls."

My mother was no different with grown-ups. She often greeted an acquaintance by poking a finger in his back and growling, "Stick 'em up." The fact that adults liked my mother was no comfort to me. It was easy for them. She wasn't *their* mother.

Furthermore, they didn't have to put up with the "Interested Observer." My mother often carried on conversations about us with this invisible person.

"Would you look at the kitchen floor," my mother would say.

"Mud all over it and you just finished scrubbing it," the Interested Observer would say with sympathy. "Didn't you tell them to use the basement door?"

"Twice!"

"Don't they care how hard you work?" the I.O. wanted to know.

"I guess they're just forgetful."

"Well, if they'll get the clean rags under the sink and wipe it up, it'll help them to remember in the future," the I.O. would advise.

Immediately, we'd get the rags and go to work.

The Interested Observer's tone was so impartial nobody ever questioned his presence. He was so plainly there, observing family life and its problems, that friends never asked, "Who's your mother talking to?" but rather, "Who's that talking to your mother?"

I never found a suitable answer.

Luckily my mother improved with age. Not hers — mine. I was about ten the first time I ever realized that having a "different" mother could be a good thing.

The playground at the end of our street had a cluster of formidably high trees. To be caught climbing them brought out every mother for blocks, shrieking "Come down! You'll break your neck!"

One day, when a bunch of us were dizzily swaying in the top branches, my mother passed and caught sight of us silhouetted against the sky. We froze, but her face as she looked up was dazzling. "I didn't know you could climb so high," she shouted. "That's terrific! Don't fall!" And off she went. We watched in silence until she was out of sight. Then one boy spoke for us all. "Wow," he said softly. "Wow."

From that day on, I began to notice how my classmates stopped at our house before going home; how club meetings were always held in our kitchen; how friends, silent in their own homes, laughed and joked with my mother.

Later, my friends and I came to rely on my mother's lighthearted good humor as a support against adolescent crises. And when I began dating, it was wonderful to have a mother whom boys immediately adopted and a home where teenagers' craziness was not just tolerated, but enjoyed.

Everyone who knew my mother liked her. Many people loved her. All have said kind things about her. But I think the one who best described my mother was that boy, high in the tree, long ago.

"Wow," he said softly.

And I echo, "Wow."

A happy family is but an earlier heaven.
— SIR JOHN BOWRING

MODERN MIRACLE
LINDA HEALY

One spring day, our clothes dryer broke. Over twenty years old, it was beyond repair, and I hadn't the money to replace it right away.

"How did your mother do it?" my husband asked.

"That was the Middle Ages!" I said, remembering images of Mother and me dragging heavy baskets of wash to the backyard; shaking, shaking, shaking until the water soaked us; pinning sheets to the line while wet clothes flapped in our faces; hanging the clothes in the bathroom if it were a cold or rainy day and draping them over the radiators; then gathering it all and dragging out the ironing board for the day-long battle against wrinkles.

The Laundromat was not an option.

Money used on commercial dryers could be saved to buy a new dryer that much sooner.

"Middle Ages," I kept grumbling.

That first day I discovered how difficult it is to stretch a taut clothesline, how heavy a basket of wet clothes is, and how out-of-place a line of wash in the backyard looks nowadays. But I discovered something else as well.

As I put the last clothespin on a sheet and turned to grab the next item from the basket, I found myself caught between two sheets. The view of my own and neighboring yards was cut off. In my tiny, timeless cocoon, long-forgotten memories stirred, memories of Mother and me hanging the wash and talking. She told me about how her mother, who still lived in Ukraine, brushed and braided my mother's hair every morning, how their tiny house had been always full of the rich smell of fresh bread, how her mother's eyes lit up whenever Mother brought the school history book home to read aloud. Through these stories, Grandmother, whom I had never met, came alive for me.

And I told Mother about a painting I had done in school that the teacher hung in the hall outside our classroom, and

Mother's proud smile felt warmer than the sunshine.

Mother told me about her first job as a court stenographer in a small village in Ukraine, how she invented her own form of shorthand, and how satisfied she was to do work that she enjoyed.

I told her about the cute boy who sat next to me in class and the friendly notes he passed to me when the teacher wasn't looking. I loved the gentle understanding in Mother's eyes as I spoke.

We never talked as much as we did on wash day. And it was always a surprise when I reached into the basket and found it empty.

Back in the present day, standing between the fluttering sheets, I heard sly footsteps in the grass. Moments later, small hands raised a sheet, and an elfin face peeked under it.

"Boo!"

I pretended to be frightened.

My young son, a late-life blessing, beamed at me. "Whatcha doin', Mom?"

"Playing a game," I said. "Want to join me?"

He edged in between the sheets to stand beside me. "Oh! It's like a fort!"

"Yes. And the pirates are surrounding us,

so we have to build more walls."

"Well, hurry, Mom." He grabbed something from the basket and handed it to me.

A bird called from a nearby tree.

"That's the pirates' secret code," my son whispered. "They're planning to surprise us from the rear, I think."

"Dad's t-shirt should block them pretty well."

"It's not a t-shirt, Mom. It's a log."

"Of course."

Only two or three items remained in the basket when my husband appeared, carrying a tray with a pitcher of lemonade and three glasses on it.

"What's all the laughing and hollering?" he asked.

"We're protecting our fort from the pirates," our son said.

"On the way through the forest," my husband said, "I saw them settling down for lunch. I think it's safe for us to take a break."

We all sat down beneath the wash and sipped lemonade and talked. And talked. We never talked so much as we did that sunny afternoon. Just like my mother and I had done on wash day.

By September, we had saved enough to buy a new dryer. But the weather was still balmy, so I pretended the money wasn't there. After all, the "Middle Ages" had their good points too, and sharing a weekly adventure and conversation with my family was worth the trip back in time.

She is the salt of the earth, and . . .
furnishes the pepper, if she thinks it is a
necessary ingredient in child-raising.
— JEANNE HILL

LIKE MOTHER
USED TO MAKE
MARJORIE HOLMES

The other day I read in a readers'-request column this plea: "Can someone please tell me how to make old-fashioned apple strudel? I have the recipe my mother used, but somehow my apple strudel never turns out the way hers did, and I'm wondering what I could be doing wrong."

Will she ever find the secret? I, too, wondered. No matter how many readers try to help her, how many suggestions she receives about the extra dash of sugar, the freshness of the butter, the temperature of the oven, the timing of the baking, will anyone ever be able to reproduce the magic formula that was her mother's and hers alone?

Like Mother used to make . . . Bakers long have claimed the slogan; advertisers have lured us with it to their pickles and catsups and jellies and jams.

Like Mother used to make . . . The very words conjure up a kitchen where a woman toils lovingly to fashion her family's favorite dishes. It paints a nostalgic picture of children flocking around wanting to help — to beat the eggs, to stir the batter, to roll out the piecrust, to cut the cookies, to handle the bread dough. It re-creates a hundred small, significant scenes — of people who come sniffing into a kitchen, begging a taste of this, a nibble of that, peering into the oven and pleading, "Something smells good. Is supper ready? I'm starved."

Like Mother used to make . . . The cheese soufflé. The nut bread. The chicken casserole. The potato pancakes. The cherry pie. The Christmas plum pudding.

Recipes we have aplenty, passed along to daughters, presented to sons' brides. "Johnny is awfully fond of upside-down cake. I always made it this way." And eagerly the young wife follows directions, does her best to duplicate that special dish.

But she knows, even when he's too polite to tell her, that something is different about it. Whatever her skills or practice, something is missing, some rare, lost ingredient that not even the best-intentioned cook can supply.

Because a mother stirs a little bit of herself into everything she cooks for her family. Unseen, all unsuspected, into the bowl goes the subtle flavor of her personality — the way she thinks and feels, the way she laughs or tilts her head or scolds. And into this dish of hers, too, go the whole measure and taste of the home — the way the dining room used to look when the lamps were lighted, the sound of family voices, the laughter, the quarrels, the memories.

Every woman who enters a kitchen carries with her a rare and precious store of her own. The flavor of *herself* in relation to her children, the warmth and tang and savor of her own household. Daily, inescapably, without ever realizing it, all of us are blending these inimitable components into other dishes, into other lives.

So that one day our children, too, will say, "My mother used to make the most wonderful peach cobbler. I can't make it come out the same, no matter how hard I try!"

Home is the one place in all this world
where hearts are sure of each other.
— FREDERICK W. ROBERTSON

THE HEART
OF THE HOME
ALFRED KAZIN

The kitchen gave a special character to our lives; my mother's character. All my memories of that kitchen are dominated by the nearness of my mother sitting all day long at her sewing machine, by the clacking of the treadle against the linoleum floor, by the patient twist of her right shoulder as she automatically pushed at the wheel with one hand or lifted the foot to free the needle where it had got stuck in a thick piece of material. The kitchen was her life. Year by year, as I began to take in her fantastic capacity for labor and her anxious zeal, I realized it was ourselves she kept stitched together.

The kitchen was the great machine that

set our lives running; it whirred down a little only on Saturdays and holy days. From my mother's kitchen I gained my first picture of life as a white, overheated, starkly lit workshop redolent with Jewish cooking, crowded with women in housedresses, strewn with fashion magazines, patterns, dress material, spools of thread — and at whose center, so lashed to her machine that bolts of energy seemed to dance out of her hands and feet as she worked, my mother stamped the treadle hard against the floor, hard, hard, and silently, grimly at war, beat out the first rhythm of the world for me.

The Essence of
Mother Love

Being a mother enables
one to influence the future.
— JANE SELLMAN

WHO'S MY REAL MOTHER?

GRACE THOMPSON

The soft yellow of the summer morning sun was slanting through the windows as I straightened the bedroom. It's a task I enjoy, and I was humming softly when I sensed a presence behind me.

It was Lisa, our fifteen-year-old. She had a strange expression on her face.

"Why, Lisa," I said, "you startled me. Is something the matter?"

"Who am I?" she asked.

A cold little shiver went down my spine. "Why, you're Lisa Thompson," I said, making myself smile.

"No! I mean, who am I, really?" Her face was twisted with a desperation I'd never before seen there.

My husband, Ray, and I had adopted Lisa. When she was four, we had explained her adoption to her. Ever since, she had behaved as if she understood that we loved her deeply and completely. Sometimes I had wished she would be more demonstrative in her love for us, but she had always been a wonderful child, and our little family of three had been my constant joy.

"Who are my parents?" Lisa cried.

"Oh, Lisa, you know you're adopted, but Daddy and I are your . . ."

"You're not my *real* parents, and you aren't my *real* mother! I want to know who she is!" I squeezed my hands behind my back.

"I don't know, Lisa."

"You do!" she said, her teeth clenched to hold back her tears. "You're keeping me from her!" She stormed from the room as I sank back on the bed, stunned.

A scene of fifteen years before played itself back to me. I was at the doctor's office, and he was counseling me on adopted children. "Some never give their natural parents a second thought," he said. "Some become obsessed by them. It's like appendicitis. Sometimes it's never a factor, but if it is, it's a very big factor, indeed."

Would Lisa become obsessed? I wondered. *Is she already?*

I really didn't know who Lisa's natural mother was. One August night after Ray and I had given up on ever qualifying for an adoption, I had received a call from an obstetrician I knew. He could have a baby for us in three weeks, he said.

Then, on a golden Saturday morning in September, our attorney drove into our yard with a five-pound baby girl, three days old. I slipped my arms around her. It was like embracing God's tenderest little miracle. Surely, I thought, she had come to us through God's providence. I was thirty-six years old, and I had been praying for a "Lisa" since my marriage seventeen years before.

The adoption papers were locked in the safe at Ray's office, but even they were a slender thread, for they bore only the name of Lisa's natural father and a fictitious one for her mother. I had thought that's the way they would always remain — two anonymous names tucked away in a dark corner of a solid safe.

But after our confrontation in the bedroom, I began to live with a gnawing fear that I could lose my precious child.

We never knew what triggered Lisa's

sudden obsession with finding her natural mother. All we knew was that she rummaged for her birth certificate and found it in our old mantle clock, then she called the doctor who delivered her. She called the lawyer. She called family friends. Even when she discovered her birth records at the courthouse were sealed, she didn't give up.

As time went on, Lisa became more anxious and insecure. Her school work suffered. Her attitude toward Ray and me, but especially me, was guarded, aloof. We arranged regular sessions with a psychiatrist for her, but they didn't seem to help. Then, the summer before her eighteenth birthday, Lisa sank into a frightening depression. "I'm just nobody," she would say. "I'll never be happy till I find out who I am . . . who I really belong to."

Whenever she spoke like this, my heart twisted. Had I been that bad a mother? If Lisa found her "real" mother, would she try to walk out of our lives forever? "Some kids become obsessed . . ." the doctor had said.

"Oh, Ray," I would tell my husband in our moments alone. "I don't want to lose her. We've tried so hard to be good to her . . ."

One blistering hot Sunday afternoon I

climbed our stairs tiredly and started past Lisa's room. Her door was closed, a sight I'd grown used to. It seemed impregnable . . . to time, to psychiatrists, even to my love. I reached out and touched the door. That locked door was holding us both prisoners — Lisa inside, me outside. "Oh, Lisa," I said under my breath, "why do you shut yourself off so? You know we love you, want only the best for you . . ."

I backed away from the door and gripped the stair rail behind me. *Love you . . . want only the best for you,* I had just said. *Want only the best . . .* it repeated back to me. Lisa wanted to know her natural parents. That was "best" to her. Could it be that I was causing the prison of the locked door in front of me by refusing to let go, by circling Lisa in selfish love — a love terrified of losing?

Lisa's problem, then, was as much mine as it was hers. If I really had enough faith — in Lisa, in myself, in God — shouldn't I break open the circle of selfish love that I was trying to surround Lisa with? There in the stillness at the top of the stairs a thought came into my mind . . . *Do you love Lisa enough to find her natural parents for her?*

I shuddered. If I succeeded, I could lose

her. But it was clear to me now. What was best for Lisa lay beyond that closed door. And it was I who held the key. "God, help me," I breathed.

He did. He filled me with resolve. I talked it over with Ray, and we both agreed that Lisa's longing went beyond the advice of a lawyer or a psychiatrist, even a doctor. It was a matter of loving enough to let go.

A few weeks later, eighteen Septembers after that first golden one, Ray and I walked into the office of a private detective. "We'd like you to find our daughter's natural parents," Ray said. We gave him the details.

"I'll start an investigation," the young detective said. "When I find something, I'll give you a call."

As we drove home, a sense of loss was already gnawing inside me.

The call came the week before Thanksgiving.

"I've found them," the detective said. "Can you come to my office?"

Ray and I left immediately. Seated once again by the detective's desk, I braced myself for the news.

"Your daughter's natural parents married ten days after they gave her up for adoption," he said. "But they were divorced a few months ago. You'll find her mother's name, address, and phone number listed here."

I stared at the name, stunned, wondering if I could go through with this.

Three days later Lisa was waiting ecstatically for a telephone call from her natural mother. I fidgeted in the den, watching the old mantle clock that still held Lisa's birth certificate. Lisa talked for over half an hour, then burst downstairs.

"She's coming," she cried. "She's coming to see me tomorrow!"

I froze. It was happening so fast. "Oh, Lord," I whispered, "don't let me lose her."

I listened numbly to her exuberant plans to meet her mother in front of an ice-cream parlor on our town's mall in less than twenty-four hours. "Afterward, I want to bring her here," said Lisa.

I nodded.

The next morning Lisa rushed off to the mall early, while I sat at our kitchen table in a warm semicircle of bay windows. Lisa's chestnut-colored horse trotted across a field behind our house. I remembered the little girl who had ridden him so skillfully, waving to me at the fence. Now she sat on a bench outside an ice-cream parlor, searching every face for a mother she'd never seen. It seemed incredible that I would soon meet her, too. "Please, Lord, help me," I prayed. "Help me to accept Lisa's natural mother and to understand Lisa's feelings for her."

Suddenly they stood framed together in the doorway — Lisa and her natural mother . . . the same height, the same eyes, the same auburn hair. Their likeness took my breath.

"Hello," I said, walking toward them. As I looked at the young woman's beautiful face, I saw Lisa's own image. And, strangely, I felt my heart go out to her.

The week after Thanksgiving, Lisa met her father and two brothers. Her world grew more complete. Her depression and her haunting search for an identity were over. Lisa was secure. But an aching fear filled the back of my mind: *Now what?*

On December 2, Lisa drove off to spend the day with her natural mother. She had talked of nothing but this second visit for days. As I watched her go, I had an urge to hug her good-bye, but Lisa gave me a breezy wave instead. *When she returned,* I agonized, *would it be to pick up her belongings?* Legally, she was ours, but what good are legalities if the heart yearns for freedom?

The hours of the day stretched intermi- nably. As the afternoon blended into dusk, I found myself slipping to the bay windows in the kitchen, watching for Lisa in our car. I bit my lip. "Oh, Lisa," I asked the dark- ness, "aren't you coming back?"

Suddenly I heard a car motor. Then footsteps at the door. I tried not to show my relief as Lisa strode into the kitchen. "I'm glad you're home," I said.

Then, a tiny miracle. Lisa came and folded her arms around me. "I'm glad I found my natural parents," she said. "I hope I can always be friends with them. But this is where I belong."

Her embrace lightened and she whis- pered something I'd scarcely ever heard her say before. "I love you, Mother," she said. "More than ever."

As we clung together, the wonder of that moment came home to me, just as Lisa had. And I recognized it as a truth that God himself had experienced with his only Son: Love that is willing to give up what is precious for the sake of another never re- ally loses. It only opens a window for love to come back . . . more love than ever.

Give a little love to a child
and you get a great deal back.
— JOHN RUSKIN

THE CHILD
I COULDN'T HAVE
ROSE SINCLAIR

"Thank you for letting me know," I told the nurse on the phone. Then I hung up, fighting back tears.

The tests had just come back from the lab. They confirmed what I had feared all along — that my husband, Jay, and I would never be able to have children. Now, as I walked through our big house, its halls echoing with emptiness, I longed to fill them with the sounds of a child.

And now, too, the guilt that I thought I was rid of came surging back. It stemmed from the fact that when I was nineteen, before I met and married Jay, I became pregnant. I gave the baby up for adoption, for even though giving him up was like giving up a part of myself, I knew I had no way to take care of him all by myself.

For months afterward, I had terrible nightmares. I awoke at night sweating profusely, remembering the squalling of that tiny, wrinkled, red infant just after birth. I heaped the guilt upon myself, not realizing that if I just asked for it, God's love could enfold me.

That evening I gave Jay the sad news when he got home. I told him I was sure that God was punishing me for the mistake I had made as a teenager.

"Don't feel that way, Rose," Jay said, trying to comfort me. "I'm sure he knows what he's doing." I buried my face in the warm hollow of Jay's shoulder.

We began to consider adoption, but I viewed it as a very distant hope. I really wasn't seeing God as a working force in my life, despite my professed belief. The truth was, I wouldn't let God be.

"There aren't many infants available," the doctor told us. "Would you consider adopting an older child?"

"I want an infant so badly!" I felt my feverish longing nearly burst through to the surface. *To replace my own little boy*, I thought to myself.

"I know. I understand," the doctor said. "It may take awhile, but we can try to find a baby for you," he assured us, recommending that we contact an adoption agency to begin the process of interviews and forms and home visits as soon as possible — which we did.

Months went by without hearing anything further from the adoption agency after the initial application process and home study. In the meantime, I immersed myself in gardening. I spent the warmer spring days preparing the ground for seed and planting. In six weeks' time, I was rewarded by a rosy rim of radishes pushing through the dark soil and the tender arched heads of little beanstalks proudly growing in line.

I watched them grow into tall, healthy plants, and I found I had a kind of maternal feeling toward them.

Finally the adoption agency called. "We have a five-year-old boy who is available for adoption."

I was filled with bitterness. "I told you I wanted a baby, not a full-grown child," I said, trying to keep my voice even.

"Yes, I know. But we try to give you the opportunity to consider older children when they become available."

"Thank you." I slammed down the phone and, tears streaming down my cheeks, ran outside.

Stumbling, I ran between the rows of beans and corn in my garden and finally slumped down in the trench that I had dug for the water to drain from. When my self-pitying tears finally abated, I looked around me at the garden I had "mothered" all spring. There next to me was the first fruit of my labor, a small cluster of green beans hidden in the intertwining leaves of the beanstalk. I longed to be able to nurture a small human being the way I had those beans.

And suddenly, as I sat there, the only answer became as clear as if God were speaking to me. Had I ever asked God to forgive me for what I had done so many years before? Or had I assumed that my sin was too great for him to forgive?

"Oh, God, forgive me," I croaked.

My thoughts tumbled and rolled. A part of me seemed to be lifted out, as if it were a burden I never really knew I was carrying. I felt God's presence caress me as I sat there among the leaves of the beanstalks, in the golden gleam of the corn silks, with the sweet, strong smell of the earth all around me. My son would be five now, I suddenly realized — the same age as the boy whom the agency had called me about. Why hadn't that occurred to me before? Momentarily I shoved the thought aside. *Someone will want him,* I thought, as I headed toward the house. But inside I knew that children over three were often extremely hard to place, and that that little boy needed a home, needed us, *now.*

Moments later, as if in a dream, I found myself dialing Jay's office number.

"Jay? Listen, the people from the adoption agency called today . . ." As I had known, it didn't matter to Jay how old the child was.

As I dialed the agency's number, I could feel more warm tears coursing down my cheeks. "Could you tell me if you've placed that little five-year-old boy yet?" I asked the social worker. "I think we'd like to meet him."

When Jay and I arrived at the adoption agency, I saw the inscription over the doorway once again, and this time I understood its real meaning for me. "Your children are not your own, but they belong to your Father who is in Heaven."

While we waited to meet our future son, those words made me realize that it didn't really matter who was the parent and who was the child, for we are all God's children. I understood it so clearly when we met Brian — a slender, blond little guy with a wide grin that revealed a missing front tooth, a child anxious for love and affection and the security we could give him.

Of course, from that day on, it was not all easy. There were barriers we had to break down in order to get to know one another, to fit into each other's patterns.

But the greatest reward has been that since then, I have felt the comforting presence of God so many times, often in the simple laughter that fills our house now, but mostly in the precious gift of love that Brian has given to us.

My life would surely be different if I hadn't uttered those four simple words, asking for God's forgiveness that day in my vegetable garden. I am so thankful that God filled me with his Spirit — changing me and making me able to be open and loving to the child he had waiting for us.

Home, the spot of earth supremely best,
a dearer, sweeter spot than all the rest.
— ROBERT MONTGOMERY

ANGE'S BOY
MARILYN MORGAN HELLEBERG

If Tom had been a few years younger the
night he came to us, shivering from the January cold and clinging to his black dog, I
could have put my arms around him and
said, "Go ahead and cry, honey. Let it all
out." It would have been easier that way. But
instead, he was fourteen and dry-eyed, and
his grief was tightly locked up somewhere inside him; so I petted the dog he held so close
and led them both into the warm kitchen.

The mother in me grieved for the part of
him that was still a child as I watched my
husband, Rex, carry in the few belongings
that were all Tom had left of his mother
and father. The Christmas-night car acci-
dent that had taken the lives of Tom's
parents had also left a big hole in my hus-

band's life. Tom's mother was Rex's oldest sister — the one who had taken over the family when their own mother had died. Now it was our turn to take care of Ange's boy.

I had been so sure that this was the right decision, but as I showed Tom the curtained-off room I had fixed for him and went back into the kitchen to make pop-corn for the family, the awesome responsibility I had assumed suddenly began to close in on me. I opened the kitchen window a little, even though it was snowing outside. Our small house was already crowded with our own family of five, plus two dogs, and our eight-month-old baby demanded so much of my time. How would I ever work one more person into my crowded household and busy schedule? More important still, how could I ever reach the brutally wounded spirit of this quiet, shy teenager who would be embarrassed by any physical expression of our love?

The children were all clamoring for Tom's attention now, as we sat at the kitchen table eating our popcorn. I think he was glad when I said it was time for all to get to bed. I hoped that Tom wouldn't notice the tension in my voice as I said good night to him.

I noticed first that there was more washing, more ironing, more mess because we were so crowded. And I was spending more time doing the never finished things — shopping, cooking, dishes, chauffeuring.

Tom, meanwhile, was facing his devastating loss with courage. Though he was a guest for the first two weeks, in an atmosphere of strained politeness and overconcern, it wasn't long before he was "flying" the baby around the house and laughing and joking and, yes, fighting with the older children. He seemed to adjust quickly to the new school.

But I knew that there were times when the sealed wound ached within him. When we made a trip to Lincoln and stopped to check the empty house, when one of our children brought out an old family picture in which Ange was holding Tom on her lap, when he was elected to the student council at school and someone said, "Your mother would have been so proud of you." At these times especially, I wanted so desperately to put my arms around Ange's boy and say, "I understand how you feel."

But somehow I just couldn't. There seemed to be an impenetrable wall surrounding his hurt; and though I sensed that the boy on the other side of the wall was trying to get through it, too, we simply could not reach each other.

In spite of worries and added work, we managed through the winter; and almost before I realized it, spring was here. I was not surprised that Tom seemed depressed and edgy after the trip to visit his parents' graves on Memorial Day. The next day was gray and gloomy, and the children had been bickering all day. So I didn't think much about it when Tom stomped out the door with his dog on a leash, after a fight with our ten-year-old over nothing at all. But our daughter followed him, and in twenty minutes she was back, breathless and on the verge of tears. "Mom! Tom's running away. He's on the fairgrounds road."

I put down the potato I was peeling, phoned Rex, and left the older children to watch the baby. I drove to and through the fairgrounds, then circled block after block, but Tom had disappeared. Tears started burning my eyes. "Oh God, *please* bring him home."

By this time, Rex was also searching in his car, so I started home to check on the children. Tears were stinging my cheeks now as I realized how much I loved this tall, quiet boy. Not because I felt sorry for him. Not because I was *expected* to love him. Not even because he was Ange's boy. I loved him because he was Tom, and because somewhere deep inside me, there was a place especially for him — a place no one else could ever fill if I lost him now.

Then all at once I was aware of something strong and solid and organ-toned that had been running all the way through the kinks and tangles of adjustment — something that had helped me cope with the added responsibility — that had made the locked doors a challenge instead of a defeat — that was making our busy lives rich and full instead of merely crowded. It was a *feeling* — warm and buoyant — like the feeling you have when your child tracks mud across your newly scrubbed floor to give you a big hug and kiss, and incongruously, you feel suddenly happy, realizing how lucky you are to have people needing your love. The extra work and responsibility then become a blessing — because there is love.

As I pulled into the driveway, the children came running out to meet me. Tom had come back while we were out searching.

I found him lying on his bed, scratching

his dog's ears. As I sat on the edge of the bed with one hand on his shoulder and the other petting his dog, I heard myself say, "I understand how you feel, Tom."

The wall had crumbled, and I had at last entered the place where his grief was. Then Ange's boy said, "I'm glad to be home." And I realized, with a sudden stab of joy, that he meant right here, in our house.

The only gift is a portion of thyself.
— RALPH WALDO EMERSON

A FOSTER MOM
KAREN J. KANATZAR

One day the phone rings. A newborn boy, victimized by drug abuse, is in need of a home. You pray for wisdom.

You meet the social worker at the hospital to gather up the little bundle, this new member of your family. You give thanks for this opportunity of service.

You carry him out in a small wicker basket, similar to the one that saved Moses' life. You pray for strength to meet the task ahead.

You settle into the old rocker, filled with awe at this tiny, perfectly formed little person. You praise God for his wonderful creation.

You realize your life will never be the same. You've made a commitment to a totally helpless creature. Even though you're old enough to be a grandmother, you're starting over as a mom. You pray for the vigor of youth and the wisdom of experience.

You're up every three hours, around the clock. It isn't easy, but it's so much harder for the little one as he struggles to free his system of drug dependency. You pray for stamina for both of you.

You present the baby before the church family to dedicate him to God's kingdom and pray for healing of all the hurts he has suffered in the womb. You trust God's faithfulness.

You eat cold meals or eat with one hand now because a little person needs to be held. You pray for a svelte figure as a reward. Fortunately, God has a sense of humor.

You allow an additional hour for collecting baby paraphernalia every time you leave the house. You pray for patience.

Household chores go on hold until that blessed nap time. Then you opt for a nap too, instead of cleaning, cooking, and so forth. You pray for grace to endure dust bunnies.

He sleeps four hours at a time, then five. Finally he sleeps through the night; it is a victory for you both. You've become a team. You thank God for his healing touch.

You see his first smile, his first tooth, his first pat-a-cake. You see him develop from a little taker into a giver. You see him becoming independent as he explores his new world via the tummy crawl. You laugh, you cry, you rejoice, and you fall more and more in love each passing day. You give all the love you have. You see him learn to bond, to trust, to love. You see him become a healthy boy — physically, spiritually, emotionally. You praise God for answered prayer!

Then one day, seven months after his arrival, the phone rings. The social worker says the judge has ordered the baby returned to his mom. She's been drug-free for two months. You cry. You remember the promise: "Come to me, all who labor and are heavy laden, and I will give you rest." You go to Christ for comfort.

On his last night at your home you tuck him in his crib, kiss him on the top of his head, and rub his back until he falls asleep. With moist cheeks, you begin collecting all his clothes, toys, and medical papers. You sit down and write his mom a letter, finish his first-year calendar, and then write him a letter, which you can only hope he will find someday when he's old enough to read. You weep, unashamed. You pray for him — oh, how you pray!

On reunification morning you give him his cereal and bottle. You hold him snugly and cry. He lies very still, knowing something is different. You give him his bath and put on a special little outfit. Finally the social worker rings the doorbell. You tuck him into his yellow snowsuit and zip up the zipper. You give him a kiss on his button nose. The social worker slips out the door with your son in her arms. You cry to God in anguish.

The tires of the car crunch the gravel as the social worker drives away. Even though you're experiencing the death of a precious relationship, there is no funeral, no memorial service, no family or friends gathered to comfort. After all, you're only the foster mom.

You take down the baby swing and walker. You wash and put away the last load of baby clothes. You clean up the changing table and close the door to the nursery, because it's too painful to see the empty crib. At last . . . you get angry and cry out to God, "It isn't fair!" You know he understands. After all, the cross wasn't fair. He says, "Be still, and know that I am God."

Finally you acknowledge, once again, that this precious child was only a temporary gift — as are your biological children. God created them. He is their Father, and he loves them more than you will ever be able to. You once again place your life and your little son's life into his care. You silently hear the words, "Well done, good and faithful servant."

You accept grief now as a friendly companion, and you go ahead with your life.

Then one day, the phone rings.

*Strength of character
may be acquired at work, but beauty of
character is learned at home.*
— HENRY DRUMMOND

A STORE-BOUGHT DRESS
MARION MCGUIRE

I looked at the dark blue dress in the window of Malvena's Boutique every Wednesday of the summer of 1936. It was a formal made of a shiny material. It had a ruffled collar, little cap sleeves, a peplum, and an artificial rose at the waist. It cost $2.95.

I had never owned a store-bought dress before. My grandmother, a seamstress, disapproved of ready-made clothes. "You meet yourself coming and going," she declared, kneeling before me to pin up a hem. But I was a restless seventeen-year-old, and I was envious of friends who did not wear homemade dresses. I dreamed of the day when I would be rich enough to walk into Malvena's Boutique as a customer.

That summer, with my job as a reporter for the local newspaper, I earned enough to buy the dress. It was perfect. I had never worn that shade of blue before, and when I looked at my face in the mirror I saw a beautiful stranger.

I had no idea I was making a mistake until I opened the box at home and saw Grandmother's face. She was offended. "Why would you want this thing?" she demanded, pinching the thin material. "And for $2.95? I could make two decent dresses for that kind of money." She closed the sewing machine, cleared the pattern books from her bed, and went to sit by the window. My grandmother loved to make clothes for the child I had been; I had made her feel unappreciated.

I put the dress in my closet and did not mention it again. My summer job ended, the school year began, and I entered college. There was a formal dance for freshmen that fall, and I told my grandmother of my plans to go. "You could wear your prom dress," she said. "It's only been worn once."

Grandmother had made my prom dress.

It was a beautiful white organdy, with puffed sleeves and a full skirt. But I was no longer the same child who went to the prom. I was a college student — practically grown-up. I chose to wear the store-bought dress.

On the night of the formal, the college gym was decorated with balloons and crepe paper streamers, and there was a live band. I felt totally sophisticated — until I saw the other girl. She was a short, pink-cheeked blonde, curved in many places. She was wearing my dress. The dark blue matched her eyes and the rose at her waist nestled perfectly to her side. The dress looked as if it had been made especially for her.

I tried to steer away, but my partner, oblivious to the problem, followed the other girl across the dance floor. When the music finally stopped, I made such a swift move for a chair that my heel caught in my skirt and twisted my ankle.

Grandmother was waiting up when I got home. Sitting on the edge of the bathtub with my foot soaking in water, I told her about the other girl.

"Well, that happens with store-bought things," she said serenely. "You meet yourself coming and going."

The next morning I awoke to the whir of the sewing machine. My grandmother was busy making my college wardrobe. She was whistling softly.

*Be ye all of one mind, having compassion
one of another, love as brethren . . .*
— 1 PETER 3:8

MULTIPLYING LOVE
TERRY HELWIG

Born in Korea, she was a little, dark-haired
baby whose mother could not keep her. But
her mother gave her a name that she hoped
would be prophetic. She called her newborn
daughter *Myung-He,* which means "happiness in the future."

My friend Denise and her husband were
lucky enough to adopt Myung-He. Denise
wanted to honor her daughter's Korean
name, but she also wanted a name that
wouldn't set her apart from other American children. Finally, she found an American name that had a similar meaning:
Hollie, which means "good luck in the future."

I admire Denise for the love and compassion she showed in choosing that name

346

for her daughter. She was not jealous or threatened by the natural mother's love. Indeed, Denise somehow seemed to multiply it. I believe Hollie one day will understand the love both mothers had in choosing those names.

What a great lesson: welcoming *outside* love for those we love. Denise did just that when she embraced the love that a young Korean mother had for a daughter whom she gave up to a bright, hopeful future, far, far away.

Love is an image of God . . .
the living essence of the divine nature
which beams full of all goodness.
— MARTIN LUTHER

MOTHER JIMMY
ANNA E. FALLS

"Gee, them's pretty flowers you're puttin' in the ditch!" The gardener from Rhodes greenhouse looked up. A boy of eight or ten and a girl two or three years younger, holding tightly to his hand, were watching him dump the refuse into a little gulley back of the garden fence.

He was a kind old man, this gardener, who took all the children to his heart. He asked with a smile, "Would you like some of them to take home with you? If you would, help yourself."

"Gee, Pinky, let's get some." Then, turning to the gardener, "Jimmy likes flowers, but our geranium didn't bloom. I guess we ain't got sun enough in our house."

The gardener looked at the pale face of the little girl and wondered why she should be called Pinky. He, too, decided there was not enough sunshine for blossoms in their home.

The children sorted among the withered ferns and faded blossoms until their little hands were full of red and white carnations whose fringed petals had begun to brown and age.

"Would you like to see the flowers in the greenhouse, eh — Pinky? And . . ."

"I'm Tad. *Her* real name's Mary, but her hair was kinder pinkish when she was little, so we called her Pinky, and it stuck."

The gardener looked down at the old knitted cap, and surely enough, there was some hair still pinkish creeping through a hole. "What about it, Pinky?"

She looked at Tad and he answered for both. "Gee, that would be swell to see your *good* flowers, if you throw this kind away. We think they're grand, don't we, Pinky?" And Pinky's head bobbed up and down on her slim little neck to show her approval.

So the two trotted along behind the cart, listening to the old man's explanation of the smooth, even rows laid out for early planting until they reached the gate and entered the paradise of blossoms — baskets of long-stemmed gladiolus, pots of roses whose buds were bursting into pink and gold, and vases and pails and even tubs of red and white carnations cut and ready to be delivered. Pinky's eyes grew wide with the beauty they beheld, and Tad's breast swelled with wonder that there could be so many flowers in all the world. The little world he knew best was drab without much brightness and with few blossoms.

"What are they goin' to do with all these red and white ones?" asked Tad. "There must be lots of rich people dead."

"No, these are not for funerals, lad. These are carnations for Mother's Day."

"I guess that was what my teacher was tellin' us. Folks wear red if their mother is livin' and white if she is dead?"

"Yes, sonny, that's right; a red carnation if she is living and a white one if she is dead. If you'll tell me about *your* mother, I'll give you a carnation for tomorrow. You can wear it in her honor."

Pinky edged a little closer to the old gardener and spoke for the first time. "Jimmy's our mother. He works at the filling station now."

The gardener looked perplexed. "Jimmy is your mother? And *he* works at the filling station?"

"She's right," answered Tad, with gentlemanly dignity, "Jimmy's our mother."

"And where did you find your Mother Jimmy?"

"We didn't find him; he found us."

"That's right," commented Tad, "he found us. When Pinky and me was little we lived down by the river in a shack. My pop, he fished and hunted pearls in mussels. He'd get lots of shells in his boat, and then he'd put 'em in a big kettle and boil 'em and him and mom would open 'em and look for pearls. Sometimes he'd find one worth lots of money and we'd have lard to fry our fish, and bread and coffee — all we wanted, and then sometimes we didn't have nothin' 'cept what we found in the garbage. Then one night —"

The gardener pushed over an empty box and Tad sat down and pulled Pinky down by his side.

"Then one night, while we was all asleep, me and Pinky in the attic on the hay, and pop and mom and baby Tom down by the fire, the ice broke. Gee, it was higher than two houses. It broke sooner than folks thought it would, and the water came down in a big wall. Our house was carried way down the river and tore all to pieces. Mom and pop and the baby was all

351

drowned, but me and Pinky and our attic floated on top. We lodged in a tree and Jimmy found us."

"Uh-huh," interrupted Pinky as she watched the snip, snip of the gardener's shears trimming away the broken leaves. "We have him tell us about it when he ain't too tired. He's told us lots of times. Tad knows it almost as well as Jimmy now, and I know some of it."

"Yeah, Pinky can tell it almost as good as me. When we woke up, we was sittin' way up on top the water. An old black crow was all the company we had. We cried and cried, but nobody heard us. We sat up there in the tree and shook, 'cause the hay was wet where the water come through the cracks. We didn't have no bread for two days. And Pinky's hands were blue and I rubbed them and she cried harder'n ever."

"You were a brave girl, weren't you, Pinky, even if you did cry?" And the old gardener wiped away a tear with the back of his hand.

"Then the water went down and we saw a boy in a boat. He heard us and climbed the tree. He put Pinky on his back, but she was so scared and cold she couldn't hold on, so he put her inside his sweater — she was a little mite then — and buttoned her up tight, and took her down and put her in the boat. Then he climbed back for me. He took us home to his house. When we went in, his mother, she was lyin' in bed and was so white and thin. She looked scared. 'Why, Jimmy,' she said, 'how can we manage with two more to feed?' Jimmy said he didn't know, but he'd found us. Then she looked up at the calendar on the wall with Christ blessin' the little children —"

"Inasmuch," prompted Pinky.

"Yes, that's it, 'Inasmuch as ye have done it unto one of the least of these,' and she gave Jimmy the bottle of milk that was by her bed. He made the milk good and hot over the little fire and we drank it. Then he put us in his bed in the corner. Jimmy's mother soon died."

"Jimmy ought to have a white one, don't you think?" piped Pinky, and the gardener patted her thin, wee hand.

"And Jimmy said we was a blessin' to him. So we keep his house clean and cook his supper for him, and wash and iron his shirts to wear to the filling station. Sometimes, when there is lots to do, I get to help him wash cars."

The old gardener took three dimes from his pocket and dropped them into the change drawer and selected three large white carnations from the pail. "Here's one for Pinky, and one for Tad, and one for Mother Jimmy."

The children took their three bright fresh blossoms and their bouquet of faded red and white, and tripped lightheartedly through the alley and up the rickety back stairway that led to their sunless one-room apartment.

"Gee," said Tad as he looked at the heap of blossoms on the table, "we need a vase, Pinky. Let's run down to the dump. We ain't been down there for a long time." And to the rubbish heap they went.

Tad's experienced eye soon caught a glimpse of a bit of blue china. They scratched it out, and both agreed it was just what they needed. One handle was missing and there was a chip on one side, but that didn't matter.

The red and white carnations that had been thrown into the ditch smiled tenderly at Pinky as she arranged them in the blue vase for the center of the table. The three perfect blossoms were put into a milk bottle in the window to be fresh for the morrow. They were to be a surprise. Wouldn't Jimmy be pleased? And Jimmy was pleased. As they sat around the little table that night at supper, Pinky begged to have the story all over again. Bit by bit Jimmy rehearsed the whole tragic tale with much praise for Pinky and Tad, but never a word about himself. When he came to the part where he brought them to his mother, his voice choked and Pinky nodded, "Inasmuch." Jimmy continued, "Inasmuch as ye have done it unto one of the least of these." And Pinky fell asleep with her pinkish little head on Jimmy's arm.

The next morning Jimmy had to go to his work, for there would be more travelers than usual wanting gas this Sunday. It was Mother's Day and men and women, their cars filled with merry voices, boxes of candy, and baskets of flowers, would be going to see the dearest of all mothers, their own.

Jimmy had his breakfast early, and when he was ready to start, Pinky chose the biggest of the three white carnations and put it in the button hole of his jacket pocket.

"You and Tad don't forget yours," Jimmy cautioned as he bade them good-bye.

They put on their best clothes and Tad combed Pinky's hair down tight and smooth, for they were going to the Mission for service.

"Now," said Pinky, "we are all ready but our flowers."

Tad looked troubled. "Gee, Pinky, it ain't fair to Jimmy for us to wear white. He's our mother now. Let's wear red. We can give the white ones to Miss Brown at the Mission for two somebodies that don't have any mother."

Pinky agreed, and a drooping red blossom was pinned on Pinky's clean but faded dress and on Tad's patched shirt.

The fresh white ones were presented to Miss Brown, with the explanation that they were for somebody without a mother.

"But," hesitated Miss Brown, "don't you want to wear them for your mother?"

"You see, Miss Brown," and Tad's face was full of pride as he spoke, "you see, Jimmy's our mother now and we're wearin' red blossoms for him."

"I see," answered Miss Brown, and as she raised her eyes, she read over the door of the little chapel the same words that Jimmy's mother had read from the calendar above the fireplace: *Inasmuch as ye have done it unto one of the least of these my brethren, ye have done it unto me.*

She gently patted the red blossom on Tad's shirt. "God bless Mother Jimmy."

"Yes," echoed Pinky, "God bless our Mother Jimmy."

Thoughts on Motherhood

There is nothing sweeter
than the heart of a pious mother.
— MARTIN LUTHER

A MOTHER'S HEART
MARJORIE HOLMES

A mother's heart is a many-faceted thing.

First of all, it must be like a cheery, glowing hearth to which the members of her family can always come to warm themselves, and from which they can go with their faith in themselves renewed.

But it must also be a cool and placid lake in the midst of family storm and stress. It must be calm and undisturbed, a source of constancy, guidance, humor, and reason . . .

It must be gentle and soft, yielding and giving, always touched by the dear foolish gifts of feathers and dandelions and school drawings and lumpy pot holders that her children bring her. It must be tender and pliant, yes . . . but, oh, it must be strong!

It must be sturdy and strong to withstand the many blows it will receive. The disappointments and things that might otherwise tear it apart, for they are the lot of every mother, no matter how hard she has tried, or how fine her children may be . . .

And so a mother's heart must be everything . . . warm and rosy, yet cool and calm . . . gentle and tender, yet dependable and strong. And though it can't be all of these things all of the time (else mothers would be saints) it manages, by some miracle, to be most of these things a great deal of the time.

*Into a woman's keeping is committed the
destiny of the generations to come after us.*
— THEODORE ROOSEVELT

THE ESSENCE
OF TOMORROW
JAN REYNOLDS

Mothers are the essence of tomorrow. A
mother's interaction with her child shapes
the way her child will treat others in the future. She instills self-esteem in her child, of-
fering an enduring love that enables her
child to love himself.

Throughout pregnancy and childbirth a
woman is driven to dig deep into herself
for an inner strength she had not known
existed. After birth, the smell of her baby
opens a mother's soul to a new intimacy.
She has crossed the threshold into motherhood . . . I have had the privilege of living
with indigenous mothers around the world
and of seeing first hand their age-old ways

of loving and teaching their children. I learned from these mothers that the natural world has eternity in it, and a mother's instincts during pregnancy, birth, and child rearing links her to this eternal chain of life.

While living with mothers from the Himalayas, the Sahara, Denmark, the Aboriginal Outback, the Amazon territory, above the Arctic Circle, and Mongolia, I saw their guiding hands and basic lives gave so much to their children.

They taught their children through example to grow confident, caring, and connected with their natural environment. The women that I met as I traveled taught me and influenced my life, even before I myself became a mother.

A mother's love has all the stars of heaven shining down on it at night.
— CATHERINE BEECHER

TO BE A MOTHER
JUDY FORD

To be a mother means you are asking to be entrusted with the soul of an innocent child. It means that you are enthusiastic and ready to share all that you are and all that you have. It means that you watch over the body, heart, and soul of your baby. Patience, compassion, truthfulness, generosity, steadfastness, gratitude, playfulness: These are the virtues of motherhood.

The true virtues have nothing to do with morality, but rather with wisdom. A mother is expected to be wiser than her child; she has to be. To be a wise mother you need the wisdom of knowing yourself well enough that you have room in your heart to love a baby who has colic, a dirty diaper, and projectile vomiting. It's being aware of yourself so that you are able to re-spond — to behave responsibly — rather than merely reacting out of an old pattern or fear.

To ready yourself, you must be willing and eager to cultivate the virtues of moth-erhood. To do so requires that you let go of self-centeredness and greed so you can fill your heart with gratitude and your mind with positive thoughts.

Give her the fruit of her hands . . .
— PROVERBS 31:31

THE NESTING URGE
JUDY FORD

The nesting urge has a significance other than preparing a clean house for your baby. As labor approaches, bringing on a subtle restlessness, and your energy starts to peak, being active is a way of letting off steam that keeps you from feeling anxious.

I also think the nesting urge has a spiritual dimension to it. While some folks insist that there's nothing redeeming about washing dishes or scrubbing the bathtub, I don't agree. What better way to express your gratefulness for your family than keeping one's home in order. Take a moment as you dust the furniture to acknowledge how blessed you are to have a piece of furniture to dust. As you prepare the evening meal, pour your love into it. Do your chores with a grateful heart. When no one seems to notice how much effort you are extending, remember that when your children are grown and have a home of their own, they'll look back with fondness at the loving energy you gave to transform their house into a home.

The nesting urge has a purpose to it; and when it hits, you can't sit still. There's excitement in the air as if something special is about to happen — and it is.

*Time or destiny may come between a
mother and her child; however, their lives
are interwoven forever.*
— PAM BROWN

A LETTER TO MY
MOTHER-IN-LAW
PAMELA KENNEDY

I know I should have written to thank you
years ago, but I was a bit uneasy with our relationship. It was still quite new, and I had
never been a daughter-in-law before. I
thought perhaps you'd think me unaccept-
able or lacking in some essential skill. How
wrong I was, and that is part of why I want
to thank you now.

Thanks for peeking in the pot and
never saying, "I used to put in more of
this or less of that." The year I tried your
Julekake recipe and wound up with two
fruit-filled leaden spheres, I loved you
for saying, "It has more body this way.

Please pass another slice!"

There were times when you watched me nurse a fussy child or paddle a disobedient behind, knowing I was doing things all wrong. You offered help so graciously, never criticizing — just one mother helping out another. When the children turned to you for aid or sympathy, you always asked, "But what does Mama say?" How I loved you for sending them back to me instead of coveting their love. In return they loved you more as well.

My gratitude is great for the times we made a foolish investment or suffered a self-inflicted disaster, and you were there to lend support. You never said, "I told you so!" or second-guessed or scolded us. Perhaps you knew we'd learn our lessons best when freed from outside condemnation.

I remember sharing deep concerns over cups of steaming tea. You always listened carefully, sorting truth and feelings, leading me to find within myself the answers I didn't know I had. Thank you for helping me to grow and learn through gentle conversation instead of sermons laced with pious platitudes.

Was it hard for you never to take sides, to let us alone to discover our own strengths and weaknesses? I'm sure, deep down, your preferences were crystal clear, but you never made them evident to us. How I appreciate you for pushing us together instead of driving us apart.

Thanks for all the times you knew my husband better than I and kept your comments sealed behind a smile. Thanks for all the knowing nods that let me know you understood my frustrations with your handsome son. You told me in so many subtle ways that you had let him go and would not be a rival for his love. I needed that in all my newly-wedded insecurity. You understood and blessed us with a giving heart and not a grasping one.

I must thank you, too, for all the hours and years of time you spent chipping, sanding, polishing your diamond in the rough — this man you grew is very much a gem to me. The tenderness you taught him, the character you helped to form, have made my husband precious and made my life a joy.

What skill it takes to make a child a man, what courage to give him up to someone else, what grace to be a source of constant love.

When my sons are grown and find wives and move away, will you please help me be to them what you have been to me? Thank you for being a mother-in-love, not just a mother-in-law.

Love,
Your Daughter

Additional copyright information:

373

The employees of Walker Large Print hope you have enjoyed this Large Print book. All our Large Print titles are designed for easy reading, and all our books are made to last. Other Walker Large Print books are available at your library, through selected bookstores, or directly from us.

For information about titles, please call:
    (800) 223-1244

To share your comments, please write:
    Publisher
    Walker Large Print
    295 Kennedy Memorial Drive
    Waterville, ME   04901

Guideposts magazine and the Daily Guide-posts annual devotion book are available in large-print format by contacting:
    Guideposts Customer Service
    39 Seminary Hill Road
    Carmel, NY 10512
or
    www. guideposts.com